Praise for
Your Best Self at Work

"The best way to *lead* better is to *be* better! Learn to lead your teams effectively and to their full potential. Required reading for every manager!"

Marshall Goldsmith
New York Times #1 best-selling author of *Triggers, Mojo*, and *What Got You Here Won't Get You There*; Thinkers 50 #1 Executive Coach and #1 Leadership Thinker

"*Your Best Self at Work* provides a thoughtful portrayal of business experiences that will be familiar to most people. Unlike books of this genre that dissect problem areas using business theory, Drs. Bennett and Dilla take the holistic approach that actually matches the personal experience. We are thinking, caring people who can be frustrated, unsure, and deeply troubled by problems at work. It is refreshing and very helpful to have this resource and mentorship to turn to."

Connie Tyne, MSW
Executive Director,
Laura W. Bush Institute for Women's Health

"*Your Best Self at Work* is a fresh synthesis of strengths, emotional intelligence, and resilience applied to leadership development. It reads like a wholehearted business novel though it's written on rock solid research by two brilliant PhDs. Read on, friends."

Brent O'Bannon, MCC
Master Certified Coach,
World's 1st Gallup Certified Strengths Coach

"The number one reason people leave a job is because of their manager. The pandemic, recent cultural dynamics, and ongoing stressors have upended a lot of businesses and the way companies are doing business. These changes actually provide an opportunity for leaders at all levels to learn how to lead more effectively. The key to moving forward will require managers and leaders who have been trained to lead authentically and who build resilience into their teams. Dr. Dilla and Dr. Bennett's book provides a foundational method for managers and leaders to both better understand their own and their team's strengths and also explore specific ways to become a more effective leader for their organization. The more leaders and managers understand how to visibly role model resilience, the more productive and innovative their teams will be. *Your Best Self at Work* creates the framework to help leaders succeed through all our next normals."

Mim Senft
CEO, Motivity Partnerships & Cofounder,
Global Women 4 Wellbeing (GW4W)

"Life is a school. Learning and influence make up the curriculum. Growth is the final exam. The key is to discover your strengths and then to give them away. This book is a must read."

Robert E. Quinn
Professor Emeritus, Ross School of Business,
Co-Founder of the Center for Positive Organizations
at the University of Michigan, author of *Deep Change*,
The Positive Organization, and *Change the World*

"As a leader, you need to know how to build on your strengths and develop your emotional intelligence so that you can connect authentically with your colleagues, building trust and high performance. *Your Best Self at Work* is a guide to doing exactly that. Dr. Dilla and Dr. Bennett share their extensive experience as psychologists, coaches, leadership trainers, and educators in an easy-to-read format that is both practical and thought-provoking. Prepare to grow in some valuable and unexpected ways!"

Dr. Kent M. Keith
President Emeritus, Greenleaf Center for Servant Leadership,
author of *Anyway: The Paradoxical Commandments*

"Oh, the places this book will take you! Strap in and get ready to combine your personal strengths, emotional intelligence and resilience to become the best version of you. Enjoy this book!"

Ken Jennings, PhD
Best-selling coauthor of
The Serving Leader, The Greater Goal and others

"Organizational leadership begins with reflective Self Leadership. Becoming aware of our mindset, how it affects our emotions and impacts our behavior is essential to becoming our Best Self, personally and professionally. Ben Dilla and Joel Bennett have written a story that can support you on your journey of leading and influencing others as Co-Creators by challenging and coaching ourselves and others to develop their Best Self capabilities. Enjoy the journey!"

David Emerald
Author of *3 Vital Questions: Transforming Workplace Drama* and
The Power of TED (*The Empowerment Dynamic),* and

Donna Zajonc, MCC
Director of Learning and Coaching Services
for the *3 Vital Questions* and *Power of TED**
work of the Bainbridge Leadership Center

"I applaud Ben and Joel for their new book called *Your Best Self at Work*. They approach the topic in a clever way with introducing a main character Sam struggling in her new role as a manager. Sam confronts many of the challenges that a new manager faces regarding work performance and expectations of her team but like so many new managers despite her best intentions, her approach is not always effective. This book is different in that it takes a deep look at the impact on the manager Sam first and foremost addressing what it is like for Sam to experience a lack of confidence, lack of support from her leaders and the level of disappointment that she feels. More importantly, the book provides the reader with a way to address this and to build emotional resiliency so one is better equipped to handle these types of situations. I also like the end of section reflection points that are built into the book. This allows the reader to stop and check in and address the important points addressed before reading further. Well done!"

Susan Steinbrecher
President & CEO, Steinbrecher and Associates, coauthor, *Heart-Centered Leadership: Lead Well, Live Well,* author of Amazon best seller *Kensho: A Modern Awakening Instigating Change in an Era of Global Renewal,* and coauthor of *Meaningful Alignment: Mastering Emotionally Intelligent Interactions at Work and in Life*

"This is an essential book from two authorities on strong, compassionate leadership and emotional vitality at work. Their evidence-based approaches guide the reader to identify strengths, develop emotional competencies, and embrace greater resilience. Read the book, master the lessons, and put a bounce in your advances."

James Campbell Quick
Distinguished University Professor & Professor Emeritus, The University of Texas at Arlington, author of *Preventive Stress Management in Organizations, Second Edition*

"I love the synergy of personal strengths, emotional intelligence (EI), and resilience. What a powerful blend to activate our best leadership skills. The story of Sam brought the book alive for me and I could identify with the challenges she experienced."

Dr. Karen Wolfe, MBBS (Syd) MA
Holistic Health Coach and Wellness Business Mentor

"Rising leaders will see themselves in the story of Sam as they travel along with her in a journey of very practical leadership coaching and development. *Your Best Self at Work* gives readers an insider's opportunity to learn and grow from great coaching."

Scott Eblin
Top 30 Coaches in the World—Global Gurus, and author of *The Next Level: What Insiders Know about Executive Success*

ALIGNING STRENGTHS, EMOTIONAL
INTELLIGENCE & RESILIENCE

Your
BEST
SELF
at
WORK

BENJAMIN L. DILLA, PHD

JOEL B. BENNETT, PHD

Bold Leader Development
Organizational Wellness & Learning Systems

Dallas-Fort Worth, Texas

Published by Bold Leader Development (BLD LLC)
Dallas, Texas, USA

Editor: Sandra Wendel
Cover design by MiblArt
Interior design by Megan McCullough

Benjamin L. Dilla, PhD
Gupta College of Business
The University of Dallas
1845 E. Northgate Dr.
Irving, TX 75062-4736
www.BoldLeaderDevelopment.com | www.YourBestSelfAtWork.org

Dilla, Benjamin L., & Bennett, Joel B.
    Your Best Self at Work: Aligning Strengths, Emotional Intelligence
    & Resilience
    Benjamin L. Dilla, PhD, & Joel B. Bennett, PhD
    Library of Congress Control Number (LCCN): 2021906885
    ISBN: 978-1-7367290-0-7 (paperback)
    ISBN: 978-1-7367290-1-4 (ebook)
    ISBN: 978-1-7367290-2-1 (audiobook)

1st edition, April 2021

www.YourBestSelfAtWork.org

Why You Should
Read This Book

- To prepare for the challenges and rewards of leading people as an aspiring leader

- To respond to unexpected challenges and difficulties in your own work and career as a result of the global pandemic, political stress, and racial unrest

- To accelerate your development as a new or emerging leader

- To increase your effectiveness in working with others as a leader at any level

- To learn more about your natural talents and strengths in the context of leadership, influence, and working in a team environment

- To develop stronger skills in emotional intelligence (EI) as you encounter challenging situations and difficult people

- To expand your resilience in challenging times and situations

- To better manage and lead yourself and others in the workplace, volunteer activities, and even in social interactions with friends and family members

- To better integrate your strengths, values, and motives to be your best self every day

Contents

Introduction 1

1 Not What You Expected 5

2 What's the New Opportunity? 13

3 Starting Leadership Development Training 23

4 Meet Your Coach 39

5 Understand Yourself and Your Strengths 49

6 Learn about Emotional Intelligence 71

7 Discover Your Cornerstone in Emotional Intelligence ... 89

8 Expand Your Toolkit for Emotional Intelligence 103

9 Deploy Your Strengths with Good Emotional
  Intelligence 117

10 Build Your Resilience 129

11 Plan for Continuing Professional Development 149

12 Summary and Next Steps 157

13 Expect the Unexpected: Going through Challenging Times 167

14 Three Years in the Future 175

Summary of Key Terms and Concepts 179

Bonus Feature: 50 Tips for Uncertain Times 187

End Notes 201

Acknowledgments 217

About the Authors 221

Introduction

This book focuses on the process of learning to more effectively lead and influence others through the synergy of personal strengths, emotional intelligence (EI), and resilience. It tells the story of a young woman (Samantha, or Sam for short) who experiences a rough start in her first role as a manager. Coming out of that experience, Sam determines to become a more effective leader. She enrolls in an MBA program at a local university and, about the same time, is selected for a leadership development program in her company.

Through a series of interactions in a team leadership course at the university, her company's training program, and working with a leadership coach, Sam becomes familiar with strengths-based development and applies it to enhance her emotional intelligence skills and expand her resilience. Sam's conversations and interactions with several people— her leadership coach, business school professor, and training instructors—help her to apply her unique strengths in first *leveraging* and then *enhancing* the skills of EI as well as learning how EI can be applied in *regulating* the use of her strengths to have the most positive effect. These new skills and more finely tuned strengths build her resilience for handling more challenging situations of leadership.

Each of us can identify with parts of Sam's experience—for example, having job and career expectations that are frustrated or unfulfilled, or struggling to balance work and life demands, task and relationship needs, and personal and interpersonal challenges. We can also learn from aspects of others' experiences that may seem unfamiliar—challenges we may not have personally experienced, or aspects of performance and leadership that we've never taken the time to consider.

It's our hope that you will read this book *reflectively*, comparing and contrasting it with your own experience but also being willing to consider ideas that you hadn't necessarily thought about before, as you're on the path to becoming your best self at work—and thus the title for this book.

We realize that at the time we're writing this, many people have experienced unexpected turmoil in their professional careers through the global pandemic of 2020–2021 as well as recent political stress and racial unrest. We believe that the concepts of strengths, EI, and resilience will serve you well even if you are in the process of adapting, changing, and rebuilding a career in these unprecedented times. Be sure to review our 50 Tips for Uncertain Times that we've provided as an additional resource at the end of the book.

We write from our own experience as psychologists and working professionals who encounter the world of work from the dual perspective of personal experience and supporting others in their journey through mentoring, coaching, and training.

Ben's experience has come as an industrial/organizational psychologist, business coach, leadership trainer, and educator working in the military, business, and academic settings; he is currently a professor in the Gupta College of Business at The University of Dallas and has his own coaching and training practice, Bold Leader Development (BLD LLC).

Joel's work has been as a psychologist and president of Organizational Wellness & Learning Systems (OWLS), providing research, education, and training on evidence-based practices in wellness, stress management, and organizational health for a wide range of organizations and industries.

Ben's work on strengths and emotional intelligence came together with Joel's expertise in resilience and well-being through our involvement in the Dallas–Fort Worth chapter of the Organizational Development (OD) Network. We are grateful for the opportunity for collaboration, professional association, and friendship as a result of this book and other offerings in our practices.

We look forward to sharing what we've learned with you as you read the book, and we invite you to share what you're learning with us. Visit our website at www.YourBestSelfAtWork.org and join the conversation.

1

Not What You Expected

It was a crisp spring morning, and the sun filtered through the many trees on the campus of Lantana University, a small private school near the center of the busy metro area. Prospective students were arriving and making their way to the business college building on the highest point of the campus, offering a 360-degree vista of the surrounding city. The downtown skyline stood out in one direction, with multiple clusters of high-rise buildings all around, with a modern "warehouse district" of distribution centers and small manufacturing facilities stretching to the horizon.

"Hi, Sam!" Jubal called out to the young woman as she entered the crowded multipurpose meeting room, already bustling with many conversations.

"Oh, hi, Jubal, it's nice to see you!" Sam replied. Jubal's tall frame and friendly face were hard to miss, even in the crowded room. "You already finished your MBA, didn't you?"

"Yes, I finished last year," Sam's friend confirmed. "I'm here today with some other recent grads to talk to people who are looking into Lantana. I guess they know we still remember the questions people often have when they're thinking about getting started."

"This should be interesting," Sam began, and then said, "oh, there's Lisa. Are you two still seeing each other?" she asked with an inquisitive look.

"Absolutely! We're doing well," Jubal replied. "And Lisa's getting ready to start her MBA. She says I'm now her full-time tutor."

Sam laughed along with Jubal. "That should be good. I haven't seen Lisa since we went to Queen Bey's concert last year."

"Yeah, she still talks about that. I know how you two love Beyoncé and her music. In fact, Lisa talks about Beyoncé so much that I did a paper about her in a class where we studied successful entrepreneurs. Not only is Beyoncé one of the highest paid musicians ever, her entertainment company and fashion line are huge."

"Well, aren't you a big fan now?" Sam teased.

"I like her music, and no one can argue with her success. My professor said she loved seeing such a contemporary example of a woman's success in what has traditionally been a male-dominated industry. And Lisa helped me with my research. I think it's one of the reasons she got interested in the MBA program here."

"So she was taking you to school a little, too, it sounds like," Sam said.

"Yeah, it was a fun project, and I learned a lot," Jubal noted. "But, hey, Sam, I haven't seen you at work in a long time."

"It's been really busy—" Sam offered hesitantly.

"Oh I get that," he said. "Our paths don't cross so much since you got promoted and moved to be with your new team. It's just funny that I haven't seen you for a while at work, but you're the first person I run into when I come across town here to the university."

"That *is* funny, and it's been way too long since we talked," Sam admitted.

"So, when are you starting the MBA program here?" Jubal asked.

"Still thinking about it, but I'm fairly certain I want to start in the fall. Both of my kids are in school now, and my husband is in a good place with his job that gives him flexibility to work from home and pick up the kids when I can't. And I'm not sure I can afford to wait any longer," Sam's voice trailed off.

"What do you mean? Are things going okay with your new role as a manager?" Jubal asked.

"It's been quite a journey, not at all what I expected, and frankly I'm thinking an MBA could be my ticket out of the company," Sam said with her face now solemn and eyes looking down.

"Well, it could be, I suppose," Jubal agreed, "but I would hate to see that happen, and I know there are a lot of others at ATA who would agree with me. As a customer service rep, you were one of the most energetic and capable people I've worked with. What's been going on that has you thinking about making a change?"

"Things really started off rough in managing this team," Sam stated flatly. "Right after I was hired, my director told me that it was the lowest performing group in the division, and that I would probably need to replace half of the team. I knew there had been some problems with a few people on the team. I'd even experienced a lack of support from a couple of people above me in the past. But I wasn't prepared for the scope of the problem." Sam paused and realized Jubal was waiting for more.

"I really wanted to give people a chance, but as I observed them and their work over the first month, it became obvious that some just didn't have the skills needed to do this work, despite training, retraining, and coaching in the past. And a few had just given up." She sighed. "They were cynical about the work, the team, the products we supported, and the company as a whole."

"Wow, that's a tough situation to inherit." Jubal nodded.

"Yes, I remember thinking this wasn't why I wanted to be a manager and lead a team. I love the company. I think our work is important, and I want to help people grow and develop and further their careers. But reality had set in. I knew that the first thing I'd need to do was remove the employees who weren't pulling their share of the load and were having a negative influence on the rest of the team," Sam said.

She went on. "It turned out to be very tough to get the team where it needed to be. I had to put everyone on notice about expectations and watch over them closely to ensure they met standards. I couldn't show any favoritism, so I had to monitor everyone's performance, which particularly upset a couple of the top performers." She shook her head.

"I removed a couple of people in the restructuring we had last year. They were clearly the lowest performers and also had the most negative attitudes. I thought people would see the difference and be glad about the changes, but the restructuring put everyone on edge," Sam said.

"I remember how tough the restructuring was," Jubal confirmed. "It was an unusual time for our company, and it would be tough to be a new manager when one of your first actions is to decide whose positions are going to be cut."

Sam agreed. "I knew I hadn't yet built trust with the team, and having to let people go made it worse. Everyone was concerned that they might be next. I also had to put three others on a performance improvement plan, based on the performance measures I'd been gathering. Not having a supportive mentor didn't help."

"Ouch! That was a bad time to have to put people on notice about performance, coming right on the heels of the restructure," Jubal noted.

"Yes, but I didn't feel like I had a choice. I wanted to address all of the performance issues up front, but I may have rushed into that phase too soon because I felt pressure from my director to turn things around quickly. He was constantly checking up on us and telling me I needed to move faster.

"I actually saw potential in these three people and really hoped they'd turn things around. Despite every reassurance and encouragement I tried to give them, it was like they just gave up. Their performance didn't improve, and their attitudes toward me, the team, and the company got even more negative. One left the company for another opportunity a few weeks later, but the other two stayed on to the bitter end, and it was bitter for them, for me, and for everyone around them."

"I'm sorry to hear that," Jubal said. "It sounds like the whole situation was a surprise, and I'm sure it wasn't what you hoped to be doing as a new manager."

"Not at all." Sam shook her head slowly. "It was definitely a low point, but you know me, I tried to stay positive and press on, but it got to the point that I wasn't sleeping well. I was constantly feeling on edge at work, and I definitely wasn't at my best as anyone's manager." She offered a weak smile.

"But now I had three open spots on the team, and I was able to find qualified people—one inside the company and two from outside. They started with positive attitudes and were grateful for the opportunity with my team," Sam said.

"How's it going now for you and your team?" Jubal asked.

"It's been six months since I filled the last position, and I still feel like I'm on the path to building trust with the whole team and putting the focus on what we can achieve together. We're not the worst team in performance anymore, but we're no better than average either," Sam said.

"My previous director moved to another job in operations, and I recently got a new director. He brings a wealth of experience within our division, has high standards, and also talks about giving people opportunities to develop and grow. That's another reason I thought the time might be right to start my MBA," Sam announced.

"That's good," Jubal said. "I'm glad you're doing this, and I wish you well in continuing to get your team where you want them to be. I need to check in before the program starts, but please let me know how you're doing."

"I'll be glad to do that," Sam said. "It was good talking to you."

Reflection:
Guessing about Growth

Early on in Sam's story we see several dynamic elements that may prove important for the arc of her growth.

First, she says, "It was definitely a low point, but you know me, I tried to stay positive and press on, but it got to the point that I wasn't sleeping well." This suggests that despite her dedication, the stress and burnout of restructuring were taking a toll.

Second, the lack of support from above did not help, but the prospect of a new director might change things.

Third, while her passion is to help people develop and grow, she can also make the hard decision to remove people through the stressful restructuring.

Finally, her conversation with Jubal reveals she can be friendly and is somewhat of an open book and authentic. Before reading further, can you guess which of these elements might be most important to her growth as a manager?

See the next section for questions that you can use for personal reflection and application as you read this book (or for discussion starters with others if you're reading it together as a group).

Questions for Personal Reflection and Group Discussion

1. Sam had several factors that were impacting her mindset about her job, organization, and career—the challenges of her first year as a manager, a perceived lack of support from above, her desire to help members of her team develop, and her transparency about the reality she was living. What are some of your recent experiences at work that are positive or negative influences on your mindset about your current job and options for the future?

2. Sam's first experience as a manager was not what she expected or hoped for. When has that happened to you in your career? Has there been a job or company that turned out much different than you expected? Unanticipated challenges? Maybe you even achieved success but didn't get the rewards or recognition you were promised.

3. How have you dealt in the past with disappointments and setbacks? Did you get upset and voice your frustration? Did you leave and start fresh somewhere else? Or stay and see the situation through to a better conclusion? (No response is necessarily better than another, but notice the trends in your own life and career.)

2

What's the New Opportunity?

(Three Months Later)

"Hi, this is Sam!" she said cheerfully as she answered her phone, seeing on the screen that the call was coming from her director, David Smith.

"Samantha, I have an exciting new opportunity for you!" said David, his excitement slightly speeding up his easy-going East Texas drawl. "Do you have a few minutes to stop by my office and talk about it?"

"Of course," Sam replied, "I'll be right over."

She hung up the phone and breathed a small sigh of relief. I'm sure glad he sounded positive, otherwise I'd be wondering what was up, she thought to herself. Why does getting called to your boss's office always raise a little bit of apprehension? She thought about some of the difficult conversations she'd had with her previous director during her first year as a manager and just shook her head.

Sam's desk was in a cubicle in the middle of the area where her team worked, with a constant buzz of voices as people were on the phones answering questions and solving problems for their customers. David was in an office nearby. Even now as she walked past the elevators to the other side of their floor, she felt half-expectant and half-reluctant, knowing that a "new opportunity" usually meant more work for her and one more task to juggle in her already busy life. She found herself at David's door before she could sort out everything she was feeling. She decided to push the anxiety to the side and try to take a positive perspective.

"Hi, David. So, what's this new opportunity?" she asked.

"Good morning, Sam. You know that I've been trying to get you in our Next Gen Leadership program, and a slot just opened up for the class starting in two weeks," David said with a smile on his face.

"I thought the participant list had already been announced, and I wasn't on it," Sam said, remembering her disappointment.

"Yes, but one of the participants had to withdraw because of family needs, and our VP, Marjorie, got you into the open slot. Isn't that great?"

"Wow, yes, I really appreciate that. I didn't think I'd get into the program until at least next year." Sam now felt a little hesitant. "You know, I'm still training the new people on my team. We just started the quality process improvement initiative, and I'm going to be starting my MBA next month at Lantana University."

She wondered if the new activities sounded as daunting to David as they did to her, on top of everything she was already doing as a manager at ATA, plus being a wife, mother to two children, a daughter to aging parents, and a sister to her three siblings, locally and long distance.

"Sam, I appreciate that you ha[...] very conscientious about doing yo[...] talk about it. From everything yo[...] new team members are coming alo[...] aren't they?" David started to explo[...]

"Yes, I was fortunate to find [...] experience inside the company. Th[...] similar jobs elsewhere, so they've bee[...] roles," Sam said.

"Okay, that's good," David confirmed. "With regard to the quality initiative, you're our resident expert on process improvement, and this project will involve your entire team. How do you plan to approach it?"

Sam responded, "There are a couple of people on my team who have asked to learn more about our process improvement methodology. I know there will be some up-front training I'll need to do, along with having them attend the company's training program. I'll also be mentoring and coaching them, but they will need to do a lot of the work to gain experience and apply what they've learned."

"I really like your approach," David said. "While there's some up-front investment in training, and ongoing support as a mentor, all of the work won't fall on you. This is an opportunity for you to delegate and help your team members grow.

"You also mentioned starting your MBA, and that's a big commitment over the next two to three years. I actually think it might be better for you to be in the Next Gen program at the beginning of your MBA versus a year from now when the courses get more challenging."

David had also completed his MBA at Lantana, a well-respected private university in the metro area. "In fact, one of the courses you'll take in your first term there, Leading High Performance Teams, will have quite a bit of overlap with topics that are covered in our Next Gen Leadership program."

that all sounds fine," Sam said and then wondered
reluctance was too obvious. Although she still felt
committed to her work, confidence had not been her strong
suit lately.

"What other concerns do you have?" David asked.

Sam relaxed a little. David was really careful to check in with team members and work with them to address any obstacles to their success.

"Nothing specific. I just want to be sure I can keep everything at work and home in balance and continue to do a good job," Sam said. "Right now I'm surprised and really thinking through how this new opportunity, as you called it, will affect my daily routine and ability to get everything done."

"I appreciate your thought process and your desire to keep work and life in balance," David said. "You know that I believe that's important too. I have confidence in your ability, and this will be an opportunity to delegate some jobs and develop some of your team members." David's confidence in Sam helped her feel more capable and ready.

"Okay, thanks," Sam said with a feeling of relief. "I'll think about what tasks need to be handed off, and we can talk about it more when we have our one-on-one meeting next week."

"Sam, I want to be clear with you up front," David said with a more serious look on his face.

"Okay," Sam said expectantly, wondering what was coming next.

"The Next Gen program was designed with two types of situations in mind," David continued. "For one, company leaders want to provide development for those with strong potential to be future leaders and advance in the company."

"Yes, I've heard that. Some people say this is a program for people seen as high-potentials in the company." Sam paused.

"Well, we don't really use the term *high potential* at ATA, but there is a desire to make sure our top performers stay engaged, have positive learning and development experiences, and are prepared for future chances at advancement as they come along," David said.

Sam nodded, remembering that David had been through the Next Gen program a few years earlier when he was a customer service manager, then moved as a manager to marketing before being promoted to a director role back in their area. Clearly, he had been seen as a person with high potential.

"It doesn't sound like that's the group I'm in," Sam said with a somewhat puzzled look. "I haven't been in this role very long, and there have been some big challenges with the team."

"As far as I'm concerned, you do have strong potential," David said without hesitation, "and I want to make sure you have every opportunity to gain experience and expand your leadership skills. Just be aware that not everyone sees it that way yet.

"The other group invited into the Next Gen program is still a bit of a question mark in terms of leadership ability and future potential. Because of the challenges with this team, and the fact that you're still working to improve performance, some of my peers and others above are uncertain about your capacity to deal with the challenge. The Next Gen program is a way of ensuring that we're investing in newer, unproven leaders. We want you all to have the opportunity to grow and develop."

"So you're saying some of the leaders in our company are waiting to see what I do with this opportunity—or if I can even hack it?" Sam asked. She felt uneasy in the pit of her stomach and was troubled just thinking about who might be concerned about her abilities as a manager.

"Yes, some leaders might be a little skeptical," David admitted. "But I've made the case, with full support from Marjorie, that this is the right time for us to make the investment in you to help you grow as a leader—to find and develop your leadership strengths. We believe in *you*."

David always sounded genuinely enthusiastic about the development opportunities provided by their company, and Sam also felt his confidence in her.

"Okay, thank you," Sam said sincerely. "I do appreciate the opportunity, and I'm going to work hard to convince the skeptics that I can help this team to be one of the best."

"That's what I was hoping you would say," David said with a smile.

"And I'll get back to you with more details on where I may need to shift some duties and responsibilities on my team," Sam said as she stood up to leave. She felt relieved after her conversation with David, knowing that he had provided clear feedback on where she stood and that he wanted her to succeed.

"That sounds good," he replied, "and, Sam, please let me know anything I can do to support you."

Reflection:
How to Juggle

Sam is going through a critical but typical transition in her career development, one that often requires navigating new feelings and competencies. While her confidence is a little shaky, she does have strong determination and commitment to high-quality work.

It is fortunate that she has the support from David, an improvement over her previous supervisor.

At the same time, she faces two big challenges: At work, she needs to guide her group of employees to become a productive team, be highly engaged, and support one another like a small community. In her life, she needs to figure out how to manage feeling overwhelmed. How can she take on the Next Gen program while starting her MBA program and also juggling her family responsibilities?

Questions for Personal Reflection and Group Discussion

1. Who talks with you about your professional development?

   a. If you're working, hopefully your organization has a performance management process with steps to address personal development as well as business goals.

   b. You may have a manager who regularly has development conversations with each of their employees. Or perhaps your manager doesn't initiate the conversation but is open to talking about development when you ask. In either case, take the initiative and plan some time with your manager to discuss your goals and potential development activities.

   c. Talk to someone in human resources to learn more about what programs your organization has for training and development.

   d. If your organization doesn't have processes in place for development planning and your manager doesn't show an interest in your development, find others in your organization who might become mentors and share their experience with you. Meet with your mentors regularly to discuss how they have developed and grown, and get their suggestions for how you might develop for the future.

2. Sam had some concerns about timing of the training program she was offered the opportunity to attend. What obstacles are holding you back from making an investment in your development? What could help you overcome those obstacles or concerns and move forward?

3. Sam's new director believed in her potential. Who is that person for you? It might be a boss, mentor, coworker, or even a friend or family member outside of the company. What does it mean to you to have someone who supports your growth and development?

4. Sam also learned that some leaders were skeptical about her potential as a leader. Who are the skeptics you want to convince that you are better than what they think? What do you think it will take to change their minds?

3

Starting Leadership
Development Training

It was the first day of the Next Gen Leadership class, and Sam was listening intently to the brief introductions provided by the other participants. She was impressed with the background and experience of her peers in the class. It was humbling to hear what others had already accomplished as managers, although no one seemed to be boasting about their accomplishments. In fact, several people had commented on how grateful they were just to be in the program.

At the end of the circle, the facilitator turned to her and said, "And last but not least we have—?"

"I'm Sam, and I'm a manager in the customer service department. I've been with ATA for five years. I started as a rep, then a team leader, and I've been a manager for two years. Everybody I've talked to about this program, including my director, David Smith, has been very positive about it, and I'm glad to be a part of it."

"That's great! Thank you, Sam, and everybody, for your introductions. Now you know a little bit about each other, and you'll have opportunities to get to know each other better and to learn from each other's experiences within the company and beyond. The connections you make here with your colleagues is one of the most important aspects of the program."

Interesting, thought Sam, I hadn't really thought about it that way, but people who have been part of Next Gen Leadership do seem to know each other and stay in touch. Something inside of her longed for a sense of community with others at work.

"As I said at the beginning, I'm Lou and I'll be one of the facilitators in this program and your tour guide for this opening day. My background is in industrial and organizational psychology—the intersection of psychology and business. I've been involved with leadership development in some form throughout my career and for the past four years at ATA."

Lou was easy to listen to, and he also seemed organized and confident with the program, which Sam appreciated.

Lou explained that the program runs for six months with a classroom session once a month. The design of the program reflects best practices in leadership development through its various components, which he summarized in a handout:

- Online resources—videos and short recorded lectures—as well as articles to read as preparation before the sessions

- Classroom sessions primarily oriented around discussion, application, and case studies relevant to the company and industry

- Monthly interactive webinars or virtual meetings for attendees to share their successes in putting material into practice, as well as asking any questions that might arise

- Individual coaching sessions once a month to provide the ultimate customization or tailoring of what they were learning to their own challenges and opportunities

"Coaching is completely confidential," Lou said, "so you can talk about anything you want, even challenges with your team or your boss. We only keep track of the number of sessions completed since this is one of the requirements for program completion.

"Your preparation for our classroom sessions will be essential to success of the program. We can only have meaningful discussions if everyone is starting from the same framework of knowledge and information, although each of you may apply it differently. Doing this pre-work allows us to focus our time in the classroom on discussion and application rather than having those long, boring lectures you might have been expecting." Lou stopped for effect and smiled.

"The content for the program is built around the leadership competencies of ATA, grouped in four broad areas, which we call **head, heart, hands,** and **feet.** The **head** represents analytical and strategic thinking skills—knowing the business, financial acumen, problem solving, and creativity. The **heart** is about connecting with others—interpersonal skills such as relationship building, listening, and empathy. The **hands** represent getting things done and include the skills of organizing and completing work. This includes your drive for results, planning and execution, and structuring the work of a team. The **feet** convey the idea of walking in a new direction, toward new goals and objectives, and taking others along with us. It reflects our ability to bring head, heart, and hands together to walk; it means walking the talk and translates our values into action.

"These skills reflect our ability to drive positive change, make process improvements, and persuade others to a course of action."

The handout contained a graphic showing the four skill sets of leadership.

HEAD	HEART
Analytical & Strategic	Connecting with People
• Researching Topics	• Expressing Empathy
• Analyzing Data & Information	• Building Relationships
• Doing Strategic Thinking	• Inviting & Including Others
• Planning	• Maintaining Harmony
• Learning & Innovation	• Developing Others
HANDS	**FEET**
Organizing & Executing	Driving Change
• Setting & Achieving Goals	• Giving Directions
• Working with Focus & Effort	• Influencing Others
• Assigning Work to Others	• Driving Process Improvement
• Fulfilling Commitments	• Selling Skills
• Problem Solving	• Overcoming Challenges

Four Skill Sets of Leadership

Lou explained: "As leaders, we need to become proficient in all four areas of competencies, but most people tend to emphasize one or two of these areas as part of their natural style and approach to leadership. This is influenced by your personality, strengths, past experience, the challenges you have faced and how you addressed them, and leaders you have observed and learned from. For example, you may feel your personal strong suit in leadership is through connecting with people (heart) and working together to get things done (hands). Or you may be a leader who tends to analyze and think through problems (head) for the purpose of improving processes (feet)."

Competencies and Skills

(Authors' Note: These sidebars are provided to define and expand upon key terms and concepts used throughout the book. They appear shortly after a term is first discussed. The sidebar material is also included at the end of the book as a resource to summarize these central ideas and themes.)

Competencies (or Leadership Competencies). A competency is often defined as the quality or state of having sufficient knowledge, judgment, skill, or strength; and competency enables one to then perform and carry out a task with some effectiveness. In *Your Best Self at Work*, we focus on four broad competencies labeled as Head, Heart, Hands, and Feet. These refer, respectively, to skill sets of making decisions, connecting with people, getting things done, and driving change. Many professions and training programs use competency-based models or frameworks to define the core qualities needed in a job or profession. Leadership competencies include many diverse qualities described in this book, including personal and social competence, emotional intelligence, and resilience.

Skills. A skill is a proficiency or ability to act, think, or communicate with a defined level of success or expertise and is acquired or developed through training or experience. Individuals may have strong potentials (strengths) that inform and shape their skills. Also, the more we use skills over time, the more they become strengths. In *Your Best Self at Work*, we discuss skills as components of the four broad competencies of Head, Heart, Hands, and Feet. In addition, skills can be either *intra*personal, within oneself (for example, self-knowledge) or *inter*personal, involving interaction with others (such as communication).

"Take a moment to think about your own tendencies as a leader. What are one or two areas that come most naturally to you, represent your focus as a leader, and contain skills that you would rate yourself as being relatively proficient in? Jot down your thoughts and capture your initial impressions before we move on," Lou said.

Sam saw others doing what she was doing: taking many notes.

"We'll be spending more time on these four skill sets in the upcoming sessions, but today we start with something that's at the core of all of them, and that's your self-leadership," Lou said.

Self-leadership? Sam wondered what that was all about. She had heard the term before but didn't really know what it meant.

"Now you're probably thinking," Lou continued, "I've always heard that leadership was about getting other people to come together and accomplish a goal, task, or mission together. That's an accurate view, but we believe in order to lead others you must first know yourself and lead yourself to be a productive member of the team and be a strong organizational citizen who puts others before yourself. Know yourself, and lead yourself first; then lead others.

"A big part of that is being able to recognize when you are engaging in behaviors that are not helping you to reach your goal and then make self-corrections. This means not only having a goal but being willing to get feedback along the way toward the goal and make adjustments."

That makes sense, Sam thought. I didn't become a leader until I showed that I was a strong performer and had the ability to work well with others. I see now that I also have to be able to assess myself, and this class will help with that.

"This is also how you recognize your natural strengths and tendencies and ensure you are growing to be a more complete leader. So we're going to start with you and your self-leadership. We'll use self-reflection assessment tools that will help you to gain some insights about yourself and provide a common language for talking about what we call individual differences that make each of us unique people. This program will allow you to sample several assessments to learn more about your strengths, your personality, and your skills," Lou explained.

Self-Leadership

The concept of self-leadership was developed by management scientist Charles Manz who defined it as a self-influence process through which people achieve the self-direction and self-motivation necessary to perform. Research identifies three types of self-leadership strategies: (1) behavior-focused attempts to be more self-aware and regulate ourselves in situations, especially challenging ones; (2) natural reward behaviors where we try to create situations that are motivating, enjoyable, and especially intrinsically rewarding; and (3) developing constructive thought patterns or ways of thinking and attitudes that can positively impact our performance. Being your best self at work requires self-leadership.

Sam had her notebook open and realized she had already filled two pages with notes. She looked around and saw that others had done so as well.

"First, we'll look at your talents and strengths," Lou said. "I believe the best development takes a strength-based approach—that is, we start by putting a spotlight on the positive talents and positive skills that make you uniquely *you*. Also, we'll consider approaches to understanding the key elements of personality and how they reflect your patterns of working and interacting with others. You'll do several self-assessments focused on skills and behavior—that is, how you act in different situations. Specifically, we're going to look at *intra*personal skills (how you understand and manage yourself) and *inter*personal skills (being able to understand others' thoughts and emotions and manage your interactions with them)."

Lou saw heads nodding in agreement.

"Inherent in all of what we do throughout this program is the idea of having a growth mindset. This concept comes from the research of Dr. Carol Dweck at Stanford University. A growth mindset can be contrasted with a fixed mindset."

Lou wrote *fixed mindset* and *growth mindset* on the whiteboard and continued, "Think of it like this: Each of us can be described as a collection of attributes and characteristics such as intelligence, personality, values, motives, and skills. The fixed mindset would say, 'That's it, you are who you are, and these characteristics are not going to change much over the course of your lifetime.' A growth mindset looks at these characteristics as a snapshot in time and believes that we can grow, change, and develop our characteristics through focus, effort, and persistence. We are applying and encouraging a growth mindset in this program."

Growth Mindset

The idea of growth mindset comes from the work of Carol Dweck at Stanford University and her colleagues. In its most basic essence, a growth mindset refers to the idea that we view our talents and abilities not as fixed entities but as expandable commodities that can always grow. This is in contrast to a fixed mindset where we believe that we are relatively set and unchangeable to any extent. This rich, multifaceted research has demonstrated, for example, that having a growth mindset actually makes it more likely that people will be prepared to change and will show a significant increase in their abilities over time.

"Now, some of you may be wondering exactly what a strengths-based approach is all about, so let me explain," he continued. "I worked for eight years for a leadership development consulting firm, and one of the services we offered was executive assessment centers. To assess leadership skills and potential, participants would come to us for two days to go through a business simulation. We started that experience with a background interview of about two hours. It was based around the person's resume and gave us the opportunity to understand their experience in greater depth and detail.

"I would typically ask someone to give me a brief overview of their career and then give one or two examples of their accomplishments in each job they had done. Specifically, I asked them to think of something they had enjoyed doing, did well (as they would personally define doing well)," and Lou indicated "doing well" with air quotes, "and from which they got a sense of satisfaction or fulfillment.

"It was always interesting to listen for the pattern of behavior that would emerge. In most cases, people were using a lot of the same skills over and over in slightly different ways. This reflected an underlying pattern of motivation and talents that was their unique set of signature strengths."

Sam wondered what her signature strengths might be, and as she jotted down that phrase, she eagerly awaited the explanation.

"Two examples stand out for me," Lou said. "First, I remember a top salesperson who told a string of stories about how he had influenced others. He started with a childhood story of how he organized his friends to clean up an empty field in the neighborhood, got parents involved to help mow and maintain the field, and organized baseball games in the neighborhood. And he did all of that when he was six or seven years old! The stories that followed were a series of similar accounts about how he had both organized and influenced others to come together and accomplish a goal or task—one that often benefited his community, social network, or team.

"In the second example, a midlevel manager shared about how she would take time to get to know her team members on a one-to-one basis. Sometimes she would take them to lunch, but most often they would go for a walk around the company's campus when they did their one-on-one meetings. In different ways, she took time each week to listen, find out about the challenges people were facing, and help them deal with the stress they felt. All of this was to help her team to develop and grow. She also related that she was a confidant to many of her friends in high school and college, and they would consult with her on ways to improve their learning."

"Interesting!" said several people almost simultaneously. "That's awesome!" said another. Someone in the front row said, "Those are exceptional stories and you can see differences between them. The sales guy had a strengths pattern of organizing and influencing, while the manager had a pattern of giving individualized attention and helping to develop others."

"Exactly," Lou confirmed, "and I share these examples because the process I used to interview people in order to discover these patterns of behavior is similar to how many strength assessments are developed. Researchers start by gathering many examples of peak performance, look for the common themes across many examples, and design ways to reliably measure those themes across individuals with some sort of assessment tool. This may include input from others who know you well."

Sam thought about her own experiences and hoped the process would help her reveal her strengths.

"Right now, let's look at the quick self-appraisal you did while looking at our leadership competency factors of head, heart, hands, and feet. While we need to develop skills in all four areas, each of us tends to have a strong suit among these four factors. Many of us have one area that we gravitate to and tend to emphasize based on our personality, upbringing, and past work experience," Lou said.

Sam started mulling over the four choices.

"Think of it as your comfort zone or the place you go when you face new challenges. For example, a leader who emphasizes competencies reflecting the head will tend to move into problem solving and analysis when faced with a new challenge, while someone who leads primarily from the heart may turn to a few trusted colleagues to talk through the situation and come up with an approach," Lou clarified.

"By show of hands, let's see how many of you identified most strongly with the head? Heart? Hands? Feet?"

Several hands went up for each of the four categories, and a few people raised their hands more than once if they felt two areas characterized their leadership style and approach. Sam felt that all four applied to her but especially liked the heart area because it emphasized including and developing others.

"This is a fairly typical distribution," Lou said. "We have people who lead with each of the four areas. This is one of the aspects I love about leadership. There are so many different styles and approaches that can be successful. It's important to know where you're starting from and what your natural tendencies are.

"But one thing that's clear from leadership research is that different styles and approaches are successful at different times based on the situation and the needs of followers. So, while we want to understand and embrace our natural or default style, if you will, it's also important to develop *flexibility*. Outstanding leadership requires that we use different styles with each of our employees, depending on their needs and the unique aspects of situations that occur. This awareness is the best place to start your leadership development journey, to understand what your comfort zone or default style is and where you have room for growth in using other styles, skills, and approaches to be more flexible and to become a more effective leader."

The room was abuzz with attendees whispering to colleagues, and Sam checked the time on her phone to see this first session was about over. Wow, where had the time gone?

Lou announced, "We'll continue to explore talents and strengths and their role in your professional development when we review your strength assessment in our next session."

Reflection:
Go with Your Gut

While a bit reluctant at first to take on one more thing, Sam is excited to have the opportunity for leadership development through her company and to have a cohort of peers of which she can be a part.

In this opening session, she learned that there is a broad set of skills that encompasses leadership. The skill sets also reflect tendencies each of us has to put the emphasis in one particular area (or perhaps two) that represent our natural strong suit or comfort zone.

To help us face challenges, it is not only important to know your strengths but to continually be open to learning and making corrections as we go (self-leadership). Going with your gut or first thought, which of the four skill sets do you think is your strength? Or are two or more equally strong for you?

Questions for Personal Reflection and Group Discussion

1. The leadership development program at ATA had four major components: online resources, classroom sessions, group webinars, and individual coaching sessions. Which of those have you experienced in your current company (or in previous organizations) as part of leadership development? What did each component contribute to your overall development?

2. What is available to you currently in your organization that includes one or more of the components discussed in this chapter? What can you do to prepare for or enroll in the programs that are available? Where might you look for the components that aren't offered by your organization?

3. The ATA program started with a focus on *self-leadership*. What does that mean to you? Who do you know who is a good leader of self first, then others? What do they do or say that demonstrates self-leadership?

4. Self-leadership includes the idea of knowing yourself through assessments and reflection on past experience. What assessments have you completed in the past that helped you understand yourself and others better? As you reflect on your past experiences and successes, what were the common themes that aligned with (or added to) the results of assessments?

5. If your organization doesn't have formal leadership development programs, consider what you could do

yourself, perhaps working with a few interested peers or team members:

a. Even if your company doesn't have a formal leadership development program, there may be individual training classes on topics such as influence, conflict, and problem solving. Find the topics most relevant for your development and sign up to take the classes.

b. If your organization doesn't have any classroom training, see if it offers access to online training modules such as Skillsoft or book summaries like GetAbstract. Take advantage of these resources, and involve others too.

c. Find books or articles on leadership you could read and discuss with others. Look up the authors to see if they have recorded videos or provided other resources to support their work.

d. Organize weekly or monthly sessions to bring others together for discussion and sharing resources. This can be done in person or virtually.

e. See if your organization has internal coaches with whom you can work or if you are eligible to work with external coaches and how to get one. If there's no staff or budget for coaching, put together a plan for peer coaching and add it to the topics you study and discuss with others.

4

Meet Your Coach

As part of the opening leadership development program at ATA, Lou had talked about each participant working with a leadership coach—someone who would help them adapt the material in the program to their own leadership strengths, needs, and challenges. Sam had never worked with a leadership coach before but was excited that it was another component included in the company's program for developing future leaders.

And when she learned at the end of the first session that her coach was going to be none other than Lou himself, she was especially excited—and a little apprehensive. Lou certainly seems to know the program inside and out, Sam thought, and that's a benefit for me being able to put these ideas into practice. On the other hand, I'd better pay really close attention in class, because I don't want to ask any questions that Lou thinks I should already know the answer to.

Their first one-on-one meeting quickly put any concerns to rest. Sam and Lou had agreed to meet in the company cafeteria midmorning, after the morning coffee rush and before the lunch crowd. They had the dining area almost to themselves and got a table near the back where they would be out of the line of travel when people started arriving for lunch.

After they sat down, Lou said, "Well, Sam, I hope you won't get tired of hearing from me since I'm one of the facilitators in the program and also your coach. That last slot in the class was somewhat on-again, off-again, so I decided I would be the coach for whoever joined the program. We're glad to have you as a part of this cohort."

Sam said, "Thank you! I'm pleased to have you as my coach because you know the program so well, Lou, and I like your style of facilitation. You're engaged without being over the top with energy or trying to just entertain us in class, like some trainers I've seen in the past."

"I appreciate that," Lou replied. "I am passionate about this program based on the talented people like you who come into it and the results we're seeing from previous participants as they advance in the company and do more."

"I sense your enthusiasm and I appreciate the opportunity to be in the class," said Sam. "But I have to say that I don't know much about coaching and how it's supposed to work in a business setting."

Lou smiled. "That's a common question for most participants in this program and a good place for us to start today. Very few people have experienced coaching before, and not many get to have a coach at this level in most organizations. Like I said in class, coaching is really designed to help you personalize and customize the topics we're covering in the class in a way that makes it most useful to you, your current job, and your future goals in the company.

"As a coach, I'm really just your guide to ensure you get out of the program what's most important to you. So let's begin by talking a bit about your background, past experience, and goals for the future. I'd also like to talk about the results of your head, heart, hands, and feet assessment."

From there the conversation just seemed to flow. What surprised Sam the most was that it *felt* like a conversation—one she might have with a friend, family member, or a colleague at work, someone she knew a lot longer than she had known her coach. Lou was easy to talk to—and certainly an excellent listener—but he also asked powerful questions that made Sam think more deeply about a situation, and he often interjected something at just the right moment when she started to veer off into a discussion that wasn't productive.

More than anything, Sam could tell that Lou really cared about her as a person and about her goals for development as a leader. The compassion he showed helped her to settle into these conversations and to center herself on the kind of leader she wants to be; it had been a while since she had felt it was all right to do that.

As their initial discussion started to wind up, Lou summarized, "Sam, I appreciate you sharing how challenging your first year as a manager was, and how it's taken some time to begin to build trust and positive relationships with your team members. It sounds like you're seeing better performance from your team lately, now that you've been able to fill all of the positions."

Sam nodded her head and smiled. Yes, she was proud of that accomplishment and pleased Lou recognized it too.

Lou continued, "You said in the short term you want to continue to build the capabilities of your team members and build stronger relationships with each of them. You're currently leading a process improvement effort that's a potential learning opportunity for everyone.

"You also said you had several long-term goals for this program—becoming prepared to go to the next level and be a director in the company while maintaining wellness and balance for yourself and your family, and continuing to contribute to church and community activities. Did I get that about right?"

"Yes, that's an accurate summary," Sam said. "I feel like I'm regaining my confidence and focus on the kind of leader I want to be, and I want to keep work in balance with other important areas of my life, with an eye toward future advancement in leadership."

"Sure. I like your insight about the need to maintain balance as you grow in leadership responsibility," Lou noted. "Now say a little more about the phrase you used about focusing on the kind of leader you want to be. That sounds like an important outcome to keep in focus throughout this development process."

"Of course," Sam explained, "as I said earlier, the first year of being a manager was very challenging, and I felt with the pressure of restructuring my team and getting them to an acceptable level of performance that I was missing the reason I wanted to be a manager in the first place. I aspired to be a manager so I could help people develop and achieve great things individually and together as a team. That was getting lost in the mentality of performance at any cost in our department at that time."

"And you said that started to turn around for you when you had the opportunity to hire some new team members and also got a new boss who was also very development oriented," Lou commented.

"That's right. I had to really think about the kind of people I wanted to bring into the team," Sam said. "It was an opportunity to re-set expectations with the team, not just about performance goals but also about how we could support one another. To work better as a team, not just a collection of individuals."

Sam added, "Getting David as a director and hearing his strong development philosophy also gave me a positive example to follow in how I communicated with my team."

Lou said, "It sounds like you saw in David some of the elements of the leader you want to be."

"Yes, that's true," Sam said, "and I think I've always observed leaders in the past—teachers, coaches, community leaders, and managers I've had at work—and I've thought about qualities and behaviors I wanted to emulate and others I wanted to leave behind."

"So what is the kind of leader you want to be?" Lou asked, using the phrase Sam had mentioned earlier.

"Certainly development oriented," Sam said, "and that was evident with David from the beginning. Not just in what he said but in what he did, through discussions we had in our one-on-ones, staff meetings, and daily interaction with people in the department. It made me realize it wasn't enough to feel that way or believe that development was important. Really, I had to also put that in practice in meaningful ways each day in my interactions with the team. It was the thing that jarred me enough to take a fresh look at how I wanted to lead."

Sam paused. "So, I also want to be a positive leader. I'm generally an optimistic person, and people have told me in the past that optimism has been contagious. I felt like I had lost that or put it on the back burner with the challenges our team had faced."

Lou nodded and scribbled a few notes.

"I want to build strong relationships with my team members and encourage them to do the same with each other," Sam said. "I really believe an effective team is more capable than a group of individuals just looking out for themselves, which is what my team had been for a while.

"Finally, I want the people I lead to have the experience of success that comes from working together to achieve challenging goals. I've had that experience with a couple of teams in the past, and nothing beats it!" Sam concluded.

"That's tremendous," Lou picked up the conversation, "because your definition of the leader you want to be reflects the kind of person I can see you already are—optimistic, strongly relational, achievement oriented, and having a growth mindset. What you said illustrates something I've seen over and over as a coach. Being the leader you want to be means that you are bringing your best self to work every day, being true to who you are, and living out your best qualities in how you lead."

"I'd never thought of it that way," Sam said, "but it's an amazing insight. Bringing my best self to work each day. I like that."

"Now that's a very important outcome to keep in mind throughout our leadership development program and this coaching process as part of it," Lou concluded.

"I will!" Sam exclaimed. "That's definitely an important takeaway from this conversation. I'm excited about where this process will take me."

"That sounds good, Sam," Lou said. "With that focus, let's also talk about which of your short-term goals you would like to start with in the coaching process."

"Hmm, I think I'd like to focus on the process improvement project because the time is fast approaching to get that going," Sam said, "and it will open up some opportunities for a couple of people on my team to take over some of my current day-to-day responsibilities while I'm leading the project. Training has been important, but I feel confident in getting that done based on how my team members are performing today."

"Okay," Lou confirmed. "So we'll focus on what you need to do to get the project going, consistent with your long-term goals and outcomes. First, let's think about the talents you bring that can lead to success with this project.

"You've shared some excellent examples of past successes, and you've had a first look at your tendencies among the four factors of our competency model. Which area came out highest for you?"

Sam responded, "The self-assessment we did in class showed that I tend to lead primarily with my heart, connecting with others, followed closely by hands, getting things done."

"How do you see those areas applying to this project, and where might you need to grow and develop further?" Lou asked.

Sam replied immediately, "I feel very comfortable with the hands factor, that is the work that needs to be done for this project, because of my experience with process improvement. And the heart is reflected in the care I took to identify the people who could most benefit by being a part of this project."

She stopped to think for a minute. "The second question is a little harder to answer. I think hands and heart are very relevant to what I need to do. But I can also see that I need to use skills in the head factor to analyze and determine who's the best fit with each part of the project, and if I understand the factor of feet, I need to be able to lead and influence my team members to embrace change and learn new skills themselves, so we can move together into a better future," Sam concluded.

"Well said!" Lou then asked, "I think you're understanding the four factors just fine, and your comments highlight the fact that most leadership activities involve aspects of all four factors. Some of those will feel quite natural, and others may be more of a stretch. Which area feels most challenging to you?"

"Oh, my, well, probably influence and change management, the factor we're calling feet," Sam said. "I see the benefit of having others on the team involved. I know it's important for them to gain knowledge and skill in process improvement, but I don't want to assume they see it exactly like I do. I need their buy-in."

From there, the conversation continued through the opportunities and challenges Sam saw in the project, her ideas about strengths and development needs in the team members who would work with her on this initiative, and specific actions Sam could take to help each of them develop and be effective on this project.

At the end of the session, Sam walked away with several actions she planned to take, and a commitment to Lou that she would observe the results and report progress when they met again.

Reflection:
The Value of Coaching

Sam is learning the value of having a coach as a sounding board for ideas and someone who can challenge her thinking as a leader. Her commitment to grow and develop is evident, but she doesn't want to assume her team members will see everything exactly as she does. She sees the need to persuade them, gain their commitment, and work together for a favorable outcome.

Coaching gives her the opportunity to think through new challenges and potential roadblocks and to be more intentional with her leadership behavior as she works with her team. Both the self-assessment and her coach offer thoughts and especially questions that help her to apply the concepts she is learning in leadership training to the specific tasks she needs to perform.

- Who has been a coach to you in the past?

- Who is a coach or mentor who supports your development currently? If you don't have a coach or mentor, consider one or more people who might play that role with you. This might include peers, past work associates, or friends.

- What are the benefits of discussing your self-assessment results with someone who can coach you in applying your strengths and developing flexibility?

Questions for Personal Reflection and Group Discussion

1. In this chapter, Sam has her first conversation with her coach in the leadership development program for her company. What has been your past experience with coaching (at work, through sports, or in school)? What were some of the best qualities of the people who have coached you?

2. A leadership coach is a person who is a thought partner to work with business leaders and help them to address their own challenges. Mentors often share their experience and give advice; trainers provide frameworks for understanding and enhancing leadership; and counselors focus more on personal issues, including mental health challenges. There is a place for all of those in different stages of your career. Which would be most helpful to you where you are today, and why?

3. Some of the most important skills for an effective coach include framing conversations so your goals are clear, doing active listening, asking powerful questions, providing feedback, ensuring next steps are clear, and providing accountability. Who do you know who has those skills and could be a coach for you? What skills are lacking that you might look for in others?

5

Understand Yourself and Your Strengths

It was time for another Next Gen Leadership class, and Sam was excited. She had originally thought the classes might be draining because of the time away from her team and the pressures of her day-to-day work. Instead, she found that she enjoyed the camaraderie of her peers, got ideas from the experiences they discussed, and always walked away with new practices to implement from the program's content. She was particularly enthused about this session because it was going to focus on strengths-based development.

Part of addressing the topic was an opportunity to complete a strength assessment. She had completed her assessment online and downloaded the report, and she was eager to learn more. Today's session was being led by Kayla Williams, another one of the facilitators for the program. Sam liked having a woman of color as one of the instructors, precisely because her experience and perspective were somewhat different from her own.

The two had bonded quickly in conversations on breaks and before and after class days, and now she considered Kayla to be both a friend and a role model. She especially liked having the combination of Kayla's youthful enthusiasm and contemporary perspective and Lou's experience and sage advice. And she knew when the two of them talked about the same principles and ideas that she was getting the best professional development.

For this session, Kayla had asked for Sam's permission to use her strength profile as an example for the class as they discussed their reports today.

"Strength assessments are a fairly recent development resulting from the field of positive psychology," Kayla said as she opened the session. "There are a number of different assessments available. Some focus on skills and behaviors, while others lean more toward values or virtues. Most have their roots in personality theory and involve self-ratings of various traits and characteristics. Occasionally they may request input from others who know you well, what we call a 360-degree review."

The participants sensed the importance of this information and were taking notes.

"A personality profile," Kayla pointed out, "would typically compare you to a norm group such as the general population or business leaders. A profile shows you where your results are similar to others and where you are significantly higher or lower than the norm. Strength assessments put the spotlight on these differences or extremes because they tend to be the traits that make you uniquely *you*. And that makes sense when you think about the perceptions you have of different people and how you would describe them. We don't typically highlight the areas where someone is average or similar to others. Instead we notice aspects that are distinctive, and we say things like, 'She's very talkative,' 'He's so quiet,' 'He's very organized,' or 'They have a lot of creative ideas.'"

That's true, Sam thought. It's the more distinctive characteristics that are most notable in others.

"Another distinction you'll often hear with strength assessments is the difference between talents and strengths," Kayla continued. "Basically, *talent* is the raw material, while *strength* is the final product we put to use. Because these assessments are often personality based, they technically measure talent—that is, the tendency to think, feel, or act in a particular way. A talent becomes a strength when you add knowledge, skills, and experience. As you grow in self-leadership, you will develop your talents so they become truly strengths."

Several people nodded as they took in Kayla's explanation, because they had heard the terms talent and strength and now saw the difference between them.

Talents & Strengths

Talents. Talents and strengths are often used interchangeably, but there's an important difference. Talents refer to "raw capabilities" or a person's tendency to think, feel, or act in a particular way, based on personality traits or other characteristics. Thus, most "strength assessments" might be better titled as "talent identifiers." Talents become strengths when a person gains knowledge, skills, and experience (practice) to help refine and develop their talents.

Strengths. Strengths refer to talents which have been developed into a set of skills and behaviors that improve a person's performance and results. Leadership strengths are personal qualities and characteristics within individuals that allow them to become better leaders over time. Strengths represent the positive potential everyone has to use, develop, and leverage their own specific talents with and for other people (including groups, teams, and organizations) in order to help others to get in touch with their own strengths, for the purpose of fulfilling some mutual goal or objective.

Kayla continued, "At the domain level, you can see many similarities among these different assessments. Our assessment groups strengths into what we call the four realms of **thinking, doing, relating,** and **persuading**. Strengths in the thinking realm are obviously focused on internal thought processes—analyzing information, discovering patterns, planning, and mapping out strategies."

Kayla saw the participants taking furious notes and said, "Don't worry. I have a handout online with the grid." She projected the grid on the screen.

Thinking	Doing/ Organizing	Relating	Persuading
Strategic Thinking	Executing	Relationship Building	Influencing
Thinking	Doing	Feeling	Motivating
Wisdom & Transcendence	Temperance	Humanity	Courage & Citizenship (Justice)
Thinkers & Creators	Doers & Organizers	Helpers	Persuaders
Head	Hands	Heart	Feet
Thinking	Executing	Socializing	Inspiring
Mental	Physical	Emotional	Spiritual/ Purpose
Discerning, Deliberative, Sees "Big Picture"	Endure, Achieve, Order	Nurture, Friendliness, Altruistic	Dominating, Assertive

Four Strength Realms Reflected in Various Assessments

She continued, "The doing realm is a focus on action—getting things done, working, being task-focused. This includes doing things on your own by being organized, efficient, and disciplined. Doing may also involve structuring work for yourself and others on a team and getting the right people assigned to the best tasks for them to accomplish. These might best be thought of as organizing strengths although they still focus on getting things done.

"The relating realm includes strengths in empathizing with and understanding others, building strong relationships and including them as members of a team. People with strong relating themes enjoy harmony and like to bring out the best in others around them.

"Finally, strengths in the persuading realm focus on influence, communication, and leadership—skills to move people into action and promote change. People with strengths in this realm can be change agents, either through their skills or their position. The grid shows some of the terms used by different strength assessments reflecting these four realms. Notice that these four areas also parallel something we've talked about before, and that's your organization's competency framework of head, heart, hands, and feet."

Strength Themes and Realms

Strength Themes. Themes reflect a pattern of behaviors that tends to recur as a person makes their way in the world, with others, and in our jobs. Most strength assessments include two to three dozen themes (typically grouped into a handful of realms, as described below). A theme may look and sound different from one person to another as that theme interacts with other themes and personal characteristics of each individual. Within the history, story, or narrative of an individual life and career, there is a tendency for strengths, talents, and skills to repeat over and over across different situations. The ability to discern strength themes often comes with experience and age and can also be facilitated through coaching and assessments.

Strength Realms. A realm refers to a particular grouping of different strength themes. Specifically, a realm is a set of strength themes that share certain characteristics and tendencies in common. Realms are often used to help members of a team identify and understand similar themes in others. For example, one person might have a theme of personal goal accomplishment while another might have a strength in organizing others to perform a task or project together. Both themes could be part of a realm that describes getting things done. One popular strength assessment uses four realms (or domains) that were derived statistically—strategic thinking, executing, relationship building, and influencing. Other assessments use a more conceptual or logical grouping of themes, such as the VIA Inventory of Strengths with twenty-four themes grouped into six "virtues."

Thus there is a hierarchy of strengths: (1) Realm is the broadest category of similar strength themes; (2) Themes refers to a pattern of specific strengths that might look similar from one person to another; and (3) Individual strengths are the most specific set of skills and behaviors that constitute a person's unique approach to work and leadership.

Kayla continued, "Now let's talk briefly about the parallels between strengths and personality. The structure and measurement of personality could be an entire class unto itself. There are dozens if not hundreds of personality traits that have been assessed. However, research has shown that many of these traits correlate with each other, and statistical analysis shows that there is a handful of factors into which all traits can be organized.

"One of the most common frameworks for organizing personality traits is called the Big Five model and is often represented by the acronym OCEAN," Kayla said as she switched to show the model on screen.

- **Openness to Experience**—intellectual curiosity, imaginative, variety of interests

- **Conscientiousness**—reliable, organized, methodical, and thorough

- **Extraversion**—energetic, interactive, gregarious, and assertive

- **Agreeableness**—friendly, cooperative, kind, and compassionate

- **Neuroticism** (or Negative Emotionality)—degree of negative emotions; instability, moodiness; we will replace this term with the positive factor of **Emotional Stability**

"Now it's interesting to note that these factors from personality theory line up with the four realms of strengths, as you can see in this table," Kayla said as she clicked the PowerPoint.

Thinking	Doing/ Organizing	Relating	Persuading
Openness to Experience	Conscientiousness	Agreeableness	Extraversion

Alignment of Four Realms of Strength with Personality Factors

Kayla continued. "The one factor from the Big Five that's not reflected in our four realms framework is emotional stability. None of the four realms appears to have a significant correlation with emotional stability. This factor focuses on a person's ability to remain calm, especially under stress, and especially when stress involves conflict, miscommunication, or reaction to other people. Some people are calmer, while others may be more reactive."

Personality

Personality is typically defined as the complex of characteristics that distinguishes an individual from others; it is the total set of tendencies and predispositions that make someone distinctive or unique. The total personality of an individual includes many of the qualities discussed in this book: strengths, talents, values, and emotions. Personality provides the foundation for our behaviors, skills, and competencies as observed by others. However, personality is a broader concept and is defined in different ways through diverse theories and models. Research on personality traits suggests that these traits can be categorized into five different factors (called the Big Five): openness, conscientiousness, extraversion, agreeableness, and emotional stability.

"It's been my observation that emotional stability may not be directly reflected in the four realms of strengths, but the *application* of emotional stability can be the differentiator that makes the use of a strength effective or not, especially in stressful circumstances," Kayla concluded and looked around the room for responses.

"Okay," "Interesting," and "That makes sense!" were some of the comments from the members of the class. Kayla had taken a highly complex subject and helped the class to gain some key insights quickly through her clear and concise presentation.

"That's why we're also going to give some attention to the idea of emotional intelligence and resilience as qualities that can be integrated with your strengths and applied to make them even more effective in your work and interactions with others. We'll be talking more about this in our next class," Kayla noted.

The session was getting intense, with a ton of information coming to the group. Kayla announced a short break, and everyone was eager to chat and less eager to get another cup of that horrible coffee from the machine in the hallway.

When the session resumed, Kayla said, "Now let's focus on your strength assessment and the patterns you might observe with your strengths that could be helpful moving forward.

"Strength assessments typically highlight your top five or so themes out of two or three dozen that they measure. Remember, we said a theme means a pattern of behaviors that tends to recur over and over as we make our way in the world, with others, and in our jobs. A *realm*, then, is a set of themes that shares certain characteristics and tendencies such that we would see similarities in behavior. To discuss these strength patterns, we'll keep our discussion at the level of the four realms, which are common across many assessments.

"I asked one of the participants in this program, Sam Denton, if I could use her results as an example for our discussion today. Her report is a useful illustration for the entire class because Sam has themes that are representative or most frequently seen within each of the domains."

All eyes turned to Sam with admiration, and Sam smiled as she turned to a new page in her notebook.

Kayla continued, "In a typical report of your top five strengths, most of you will have strengths identified in two or three of the four realms we discussed. Some of you will have strengths in all four realms, like Sam does in her results, and a few may have all of their strengths in a single realm.

"I want to emphasize that no pattern is better than another," Kayla noted. "What's important is to look at your own themes in the context of others on the same team to see how your strengths can balance and support one another.

"Each of you will also have a dominant realm among your top strengths. You may have two to five strengths in that realm. In Sam's case, although she had one theme in each of the four realms we've identified, she had two themes in relating, which would make that her dominant realm."

"That's Sam all right!" shouted Dorian, another member of the class. "It's really easy to get to know Sam, and she shows a real interest in each of us."

"Thanks for the confirmation, Dorian," Kayla said, adding, "so we see those strengths in action by the way someone works and interacts with others.

"I should also note that some of you may have two themes in each of two realms (and a fifth theme in a different realm), meaning that you have a tie between two domains being dominant for you. You can resolve this in one of several ways: first, you can look at the rank order of themes to see if one realm would be placed higher than the other; or, second, you can decide based on your gut or intuition which realm seems more dominant for you; or finally you might explore both realms as being equally important in understanding your strengths profile."

Kayla said, "Let's unpack your strengths profile a little further by looking at each of the four realms reflected in the assessment you completed. We'll start with the thinking strengths, which are strengths involving thought, reflection, and analysis. This report shows Sam's love of learning is one of her key strengths. It's also one of the most common across our class and in the larger set of results for everyone who has taken this assessment. Those of you with this strength appreciate almost any opportunity to learn something new, to discover new information, or to build new skills.

"The second realm is the doing strengths, and Sam's report show that she's very achievement oriented. In other words, she likes to set and achieve challenging goals and often works with others for a mutual sense of accomplishment. Again, this is one of the most common themes, both in this group and in results from others across the country and around the world who have taken the assessment.

"In the relating realm, I've already mentioned that Sam had two of her top five strength themes. Her results show that she is naturally empathetic with others and that she builds deep, lasting relationships with others on a one-to-one basis. This pattern of relating is one of the most common strength themes, and it's shared by many of you here today."

Sam was not surprised to see her strengths building. She was comfortable sharing her results, and she guessed that others shared some of her themes as they nodded or looked in her direction.

"Finally in the realm of persuading, Sam's report shows that communicating with others is one of her key strength themes. People with this theme have the ability to express their thoughts in a variety of ways, from informal conversation to formal presentations as well as writing. This theme, along with others in the persuading realm, can be helpful in getting a team moving together in the same direction and getting the resources and support the team needs from others in an organization.

"I will mention that persuading strengths tend to occur at a lower frequency in the population than strengths in the other three realms. We said this realm correlates with the personality factor of extraversion. Many people are extraverted in their interactions with others; however," and Kayla paused for effect, "the *trait* within the extraversion factor that is most indicative of persuading strengths is the trait of assertiveness. Of course, not every extravert is highly assertive. And in many cultures and organizations, it may be less socially acceptable to be assertive, which may be the reason these strengths are not seen as frequently as strengths in the other realms."

A lot to think about, Sam reflected.

"In summary," Kayla said, "we looked at the four realms of strengths. We saw in Sam's profile specific themes in each of the four realms that were some of the most frequent results in strength assessment data. Hopefully you could identify with one or more of Sam's strength themes, or at least with the realms in which they fell."

Classmates were nodding their heads.

"You may have other themes in the same realms that sounded similar in some ways to the strengths we discussed, yet they are distinctive in other ways. And instead of having strengths in all four realms, your themes may cluster in three, two, or even just one of the four realms. No pattern is better than another, but people do vary in the depth and breadth of their strength profile across the four realms. What's important is, one, to understand the realms where you have strengths; two, decide what is your most dominant realm; and, three, determine where you need others to round out the strengths profile when you're a part of a team."

As the fact-filled session began to wrap up, Kayla concluded, "Remember that it's not just a matter of understanding your own strengths. In organizations today, we most often work in the context of teams, crews, departments, projects, and relationships. One objective of this leadership development class is to understand your strengths in relation to others. Teams need a diversity of strengths. Great teams have a mix of people with many different strength themes. The best leaders learn to appreciate the value of all of the strengths that each of the team members has, so they can work together for greater effectiveness as a team.

"Your strength profile can affect everything you do as a team member and as a leader. More than any other standard assessment of which I'm aware, a strength assessment shows what makes you uniquely *you*. In order to be the best leader that you can be, you'll want to focus and center yourself in your strengths. We'll continue to refer back to your strengths as we explore a variety of leadership skills in our upcoming classes," Kayla said as she concluded the module. "And thanks, Sam, for letting me share your profile as an example."

Reflection:
Know Yourself

Sam and her cohort learn about four realms of strengths that emerge from a variety of research on personality and human behavior and are reflected in a wide range of strength assessments that are available. These talents (the raw material) and strengths (the refined product) are also reflected in personality theory.

The four realms of strengths correlate with four of the five major factors of personality reflected in Big Five personality assessments. Effective leaders show competency in three areas: they find confidence and center themselves on their own unique strengths; at the same time, they remain aware of their potential weaknesses and how they might impact performance; and they also recognize and help bring out the strengths of others on their team, especially complementary strengths.

Be sure to complete one or more of the available strength assessments to gain understanding of the areas that are hard-wired in you. A sample strength assessment, focusing on the broad level of the four realms of strength, is provided in the next section.

Knowing your strengths and how they work together to produce success for you is fundamental to being able to develop and enhance new skills and behavior. The next chapter will introduce the concept of emotional intelligence before we explore how the four realms of strength link to human emotions and interactions.

Your Strengths:
Quick Self-Assessment

There are two parts to this assessment. [Note: You may also download this assessment at www.YourBestSelfAtWork.org.]

Part 1. Your Strength Profile: Initial Exploration

Each of the following eight statements has four options for responding. Please select the option that best describes you. Mark that off in the grid at the end of the eight statements. If you have difficulty deciding between two statements, select one as your best description and you can also select the second best as well.

1. When faced with an unexpected challenge in meeting deadlines at work or school, my tendency is to

   a. Focus on a plan for efficiency
   b. Roll up my sleeves and finish what I set out to do
   c. Ask or work with others to divide up the work
   d. Enjoy the challenge itself and learn from it

2. As I look toward the future, the ideal career (or next step) for me would include more opportunity

    a. For study and research
    b. To accomplish important goals
    c. To network and build professional relationships
    d. To direct others on completing a project

3. When people come to me for suggestions, advice, or ideas, it tends to be for

    a. Helping them with information or to analyze the situation
    b. Helping them find a way to work through a challenge
    c. Listening and support
    d. Solve problems they have with influencing others

4. When left alone with my own thoughts, my mind generally goes to

    a. Thinking and analysis
    b. My to-do list and what I need to get done next
    c. People I need to connect to
    d. How I can get others to do what needs to get done

5. From the list below, select the adjective that people who know you well would most likely use to describe you

    a. Analytical
    b. Person of action
    c. Social
    d. Influential

6. From the list below, select the type of person or hero that you aspire to be most like

    a. An inventor who designed a successful patent

    b. An explorer who discovered a new land or vista

    c. A teacher who helped many grow

    d. A contributor to an agency that improved the world

7. Which of the types of books or magazines do you most prefer to browse if you have the time?

    a. Science, new ideas, new discoveries

    b. Do-it-yourself guides, manuals, cookbooks

    c. Social activities, community happenings, meet-ups

    d. Success in business or self-improvement

8. In which type of organization would you be most likely to thrive and advance in your career?

    a. Think tank where I would work with data analytics or new technology

    b. Manufacturing or construction where I get to use my hands every day

    c. Service or customer-oriented where I interact with others

    d. Any job where I show success in influencing others (for example, sales, marketing, teaching)

Tabulating Your Responses

Place a mark that corresponds to your most preferred response to each of the eight items. After you make all marks, please tally the total of marks for each one. If you had difficulty and could not decide between your top two answers, please make a different mark for your second choice and include that as a "consideration" in your tally.

Item	Answered a	Answered b	Answered c	Answered d
1				
2				
3				
4				
5				
6				
7				
8				
Total				

Tally your totals in the columns. Note which columns have more marks to identify strength tendencies. The columns represent the four realms: (a) Thinking, (b) Doing, (c) Relating, and (d) Persuading.

Reflect on your responses and totals. There are several possible patterns:

- A particular strength realm (column) stood out clearly above the others.

- Your responses suggested that you have a tie between two top realms.

- Your responses indicate that you have a range of strengths with similar scores across three or four columns.

Part 2. Determining Your Strength Order

Regardless of your pattern in Part 1, this next step can be helpful in further clarifying your strengths. First, read through each of the sections below. Number them from 1 to 4 based on how much you resonate, like, or feel that the section describes you.

RANK ORDER	
	I am someone who takes time to think through my actions, reflect on subjects I have read about, recall people and events, and make an effort to gain greater knowledge, insight, and understanding of the world around me.
	I am someone who prefers to dive into tasks, reach goals, and feel a sense of accomplishment from day to day. I like staying busy, and also prefer to organize my schedule and tasks as a way to achieve outcomes that I set out to achieve.
	I enjoy supporting others and finding ways to get people to get along, work together toward common goals, and feel part of a team or community. This means that I like to listen, make connections, and communicate.
	I am most satisfied when I can get others to do, think, or feel something because of something I said or did. I am fairly certain that others find me persuasive, influential, motivating, and maybe even inspiring at times.

Note: In order, the four sections represent (a) Thinking, (b) Doing, (c) Relating, and (d) Persuading.

FINAL STEP: As you review the results from Part 1 and Part 2, what conclusions do you draw about your profile and your dominant realm(s)?

Questions for Personal Reflection and Group Discussion

1. A number of different talent or strength assessments are available today. Some are free, while others have reasonable fees similar to other validated assessment tools. Which ones have you completed? Which of them interest you? (You can find more information about these assessments in the End Notes.)

    - Gallup's CliftonStrengths® assessment (previously StrengthsFinder®)

    - The VIA Inventory of Strengths (VIA-IS), formerly known as the Values in Action Inventory

    - Strengths Profile (previously known as the Realise2 Inventory)

    - StandOut (and the updated StandOut 2.0) developed by Marcus Buckingham

    - Strengthscope®

    - Qualitative 360/Reflected Best Self Exercise™

2. The chapter discussed four typical realms in which strengths tend to cluster: thinking, doing, relating, and persuading. How many of the four realms are represented in your results? Which is your dominant realm of strengths from your results? (Remember, no pattern is better than another; it's a question of how your strengths fit the demands of a situation, such as your job context, and the people with whom you interact.)

3. Think back to some of your peak experiences and most fulfilling moments in the past. What were you doing in those situations that brought satisfaction and fulfillment? How are your strengths reflected in those examples?

6

Learn about
Emotional Intelligence

Sam arrived on campus early for her first class at Lantana University, where she was beginning work on her MBA. With everything else that was happening in her life and her work, she decided to set a steady pace with this program, two courses per term, that would allow her to finish the program in two years. In the first semester she was taking Financial Accounting and Effective Team Leadership. She thought the balance of a numbers class and one on so-called soft skills would provide some balance and help ensure success.

Her leadership class was being taught by Dr. Marybeth Lambert. The professor's online bio said that she was the professor who designed this class and that she teaches it regularly.

"Welcome to our class!" Dr. Lambert said cheerfully when she walked into the classroom of twenty students. "I know many of you are just starting your MBA or another specialized master's degree in business. If that's the case, welcome to the university also."

The group of students, of various ages, with Sam on the older end of the bunch, murmured hellos and got their laptops out for notetaking.

"First let me say that you can call me Marybeth if you're comfortable being on a first name basis with your professor. If you prefer a title, many of my past students have called me Dr. Marybeth."

Several students smiled and nodded, appreciating the invitation to use a less formal title for their professor.

Dr. Marybeth continued, "I originally designed this class ten years ago, based on what local hiring managers told us they wanted to see in graduates of the MBA and other degree programs. A large number of those topics come under the theme of emotional intelligence, and we'll be spending five of our twelve classes exploring the skills of EI, starting tonight with an overview."

Sam had heard the term *emotional intelligence* at her company for years and knew it would be a topic in the Next Gen Leadership program. It seemed even more important after hearing what her professor said about hiring managers who identified the skills they wanted in new MBAs.

"Each of you has the emotional intelligence book as one of several textbooks we use in this class, and the book provided you with the opportunity to complete an online self-assessment of your own emotional intelligence skills. So let's take a look at your results and what they mean.

"Let's start with the model of emotional intelligence, so we can understand its components as many authors including Dr. Daniel Goleman have discussed them. You see that emotional intelligence or EI is first divided into two components: personal competence and social competence. Personal competence is about knowing and managing yourself as an individual, while social competence is about recognizing emotions in others and managing your interactions with them."

Sam found the graphic of the components of EI in her course materials and clicked on it so she could view the areas on her laptop during the lecture.

Components of Emotional Intelligence	Self Personal Competence	Others Social Competence
Awareness ("What I See")	Self-Awareness	Social Awareness
Management ("What I Do")	Self-Management	Relationship Management

Four Components of Emotional Intelligence (EI)

"Each of these components is further divided into awareness of emotions (in yourself and others), and management, which refers to the actions you take in response to your awareness— that is, the management of yourself and your relationships in the context of emotions," the professor explained.

"These two divisions of EI together result in four parts, which will be the focus of the rest of your report as well as our discussions in class. We have self-awareness and self-management as the two aspects of personal competence, and social awareness and relationship management as the two aspects of social competence."

Emotional Intelligence (EI)

EI refers to a set of skills and behaviors that can be developed and improved in the areas of understanding and navigating the emotional experiences in oneself and others. EI is the capacity to be aware of, control, and express one's emotions, and to handle interpersonal relationships judiciously and empathetically. EI has four components: self-awareness, self-management, social awareness, and relationship management. Emotional intelligence supports us in being our best self at work, and, as emotionally intelligent leaders, we can support and even help bring out the best self of others at work.

"Professor, I have a question," said one of Sam's fellow students, with his hand up. "If the action component of our self-awareness is self-management, why don't we call the action component of social awareness managing others? Isn't that what we're doing?"

"Well, that's a good point," she said, "given how this model is structured. It seems like it would be a better parallel to say we manage others based on our awareness of their emotions, just like we manage ourselves based on self-awareness of our own emotions, right? But in reality, we can't control the thoughts, feelings, or behaviors of others, can we?"

"No, I guess we can't really do that. On most days, I have enough to handle trying to manage my own emotions," he said and others laughed, nodding their heads in agreement.

Another student spoke up and said, "At my company we're told to check our emotions at the door and not let them affect our work or how we interact with others."

"Not to sound too much like an armchair psychologist," said Dr. Marybeth, "but how's that working for you and others in your company?"

"Well, to tell the truth, nobody seems to worry about it too much, unless there's something emotional going on with someone that makes our boss uncomfortable, and then we're reminded to leave that stuff at home. As employees we tend to look out for each other and make sure we support each other if something tough is going on outside of work."

Dr. Marybeth smiled and said, "I believe what you and your team members do for each other is a best practice on a team and reflects the fact that, as people, we are both rational and emotional. We can't leave our emotions at the door at work any more than we can stop our brains from thinking about a problem when it presents itself. Emotion does enter into our interactions at work whether we like it or not. I can't manage the emotions in you, and you can't manage the emotions in me, but we can manage our relationship, our communication and interaction, in a way that aims to positively influence each other in the context of emotional situations. We'll talk about this more when we get to relationship management as a topic later in the course."

She turned to her notes. "This is a good time to note that in this class we're taking a mixed approach to emotional intelligence. As I said before, EI has been defined in different ways by various authors and researchers. Some focus on a set of personality traits, attitudes, and behaviors in how they define EI—what is often called a trait-based approach. Others take a perspective that looks at the skills and abilities that make up EI, focusing on behaviors that we can observe and skills that we can improve. We believe there's value in both perspectives. Each of us has a natural set of traits and characteristics that predisposes us to a natural level of awareness of emotions in ourselves and others. However, EI is also a set of skills and behaviors that can be developed and improved," the professor said as she flipped the PowerPoint to show the next slide.

"Let me share a chart we'll be using over the next several class sessions as we explore each of the four components of EI. It lists some of the key skills or competencies that make up each aspect of EI. It should help you see why we place such strong emphasis on EI in a class on leadership. This list of skills is a broad set of competencies in how we lead ourselves and others. There are other aspects of business knowledge and problem solving that are important, but EI represents a broad set of skills in how we interact with situations and other people."

Skills of Emotional Intelligence	Self	Others
Awareness	**Self-Awareness** • *Emotional awareness* • *Self-assessment* • *Self-confidence*	**Social Awareness** • *Empathy* • *Developing others* • *Political awareness*
Management	**Self-Management** • *Self-control* • *Adaptability* • *Motivation*	**Relationship Management** • *Communication & influence* • *Conflict management* • *Teamwork & collaboration*

The Skills of Emotional Intelligence (EI)

"Now let's continue looking at your report. You'll see that you get a numerical score between 0 and 100 for each of the four components of EI. The report describes the meaning of different ranges on the 100-point scale. While this can be helpful to know, I'd encourage you to focus primarily on what your own highest and lowest scores are. The truth is that we all fill out surveys in a different way. For example, some of us rarely use extreme scores on either end of the scale, while others use the entire scale. That tendency to respond in a narrow or wide range (or even a tendency to assign higher or lower scores relative to others) may influence where you came out with regard to the ranges described," Dr. Marybeth said.

Sam pulled out her report for reference. She had taken the assessment online before the first day of class, and now she was eager to see what the scores all meant.

"The report provides all of the numerical scores from your assessment, and you'll see scores for each of the components plus averages for personal and social competence, and an overall score for your emotional intelligence. Our focus will be more on the parts and less on the overall number, because we believe almost everyone has room to improve when it comes to emotional intelligence.

"Take a moment to look at your scores," Dr. Marybeth suggested. "In terms of the range in which your scores fall, does the description fit what you believe to be your EI skills? Which of the four components is your highest score? This is likely to be a strength to build upon. Which score is lowest? This may show a need for development."

"Dr. Marybeth, my scores were really close to each other." Sam was almost surprised to hear herself asking the question out loud in front of the rest of the class, but she really wanted to know the answer. "Is a difference of two or three points out of a hundred points on each scale considered to be a big difference?"

"Sam, I'm sure you're not the only person with that question, and it goes back to the fact that each of us fills out these surveys differently, and we interpret the results differently. You may feel like a difference of a few points is important, while someone else might feel they scored essentially the same.

"That's why I say that your lowest score *may* show a need for development, because the other question we always want to ask with respect to EI is what practical challenges do you face in your work and your life individually and in your interactions with others? You might feel, for example, because of some tough challenges ahead at work or other aspects of your life that self-management skills are going to be most important to you, even if that score is not your lowest. It might even be your highest score and still be the one with the biggest potential payoff for you. Bottom line: understand the numbers but use your results in a way that makes sense for you and your situation."

"Okay, thank you," Sam replied, "because I don't think my lowest score is the area that needs the most attention, based on what I know about myself and feedback I've gotten from my boss and others. We have some issues going on at work that make me believe relationship management will be the most important aspect for me over the next few months, but that wasn't my lowest score."

"Excellent!" Dr. Marybeth replied enthusiastically. "I really appreciate that as an example of self-reflection and taking time to interpret your results in a broader context of self-awareness, feedback, and situational considerations. This sort of self-reflection is a key part of self-leadership."

"Thank you," Sam replied to her instructor. "I'm part of a leadership program at work called Next Gen Leadership, and we just talked about self-leadership as a starting point for our leadership development."

"Sounds like a great opportunity for you, and self-reflection is the first step toward real change and growth," Dr. Marybeth said in agreement. "Another part of self-leadership is being open to and being able to make self-corrections so you can do a better job of reaching your goals.

"Now let me also point out that your EI report also provides development suggestions or strategies to enhance the areas on which you scored the lowest. The report identifies the dimension of EI on which you scored the lowest and the individual items or behaviors where you scored the lowest. For each of these, there's a strategy to help you improve that specific behavior."

The class was taking notes as the professor explained the process.

"As an example, and in the interest of full disclosure as your instructor, I'll talk about my own report. My lowest score was in relationship management, and my report shows that the items which brought my score down the most had to do with handling conflict, openness with others, and demonstrating sensitivity to others' feelings. I'm given three strategies, one paired to each of these items or behaviors.

"For conflict, for example, I see that one strategy is to tackle a tough conversation. For openness, I see that a strategy is to explain your decisions, don't just make them, and for sensitivity, the strategy is to acknowledge the other person's feelings. I can go to the pages listed in the book for more information, or I can simply review the actions summarized in the report.

"Now I've been teaching about EI for a number of years, but my results were accurate. For example, I know that I tend to avoid conflict. And at the time I first took this assessment about five years ago, there was a particular conflict that I had put off dealing with, and it was just lurking out there, in the shadows. My report brought it into the light so I couldn't ignore any longer that I had a conflict that needed resolving, and part of the problem was that I didn't want to deal with it."

Many in the group were nodding their heads as if understanding the situation.

Dr. Marybeth explained, "The strategy for tackling a tough conversation gave me some very practical steps for being able to do that. For example, it says start with agreement or the common ground that you share with others. In my situation, where I had a conflict with one of my peers on the faculty, this meant starting the conversation by noting that we both put high value on serving the needs of our students. Starting from that common perspective was an invitation to delve into our differences and gave me confidence that we'd be able to find a solution that worked best for everyone, especially for our students.

"The strategy presented in my report gave a number of other practical actions that I was able to incorporate in having this conversation with my colleague, such as trying first to understand their perspective, explaining my thoughts and ideas, moving the conversation forward with a specific next step, and keeping in touch on the issue. By using those suggestions, I was able to address the conflict with my peer, and I have to tell you, it wasn't as difficult as I had envisioned it being. We were able to resolve that disagreement and have since worked on a couple of projects together."

"Thanks, professor, for your example," called out Caitlyn from the back of the room. "I'm taking a lot of notes because conflict is a big challenge for me too."

"I'm sure you and I are not alone in that challenge," Dr. Marybeth said. "In this class you'll each be putting together a learning plan of specific areas where you want to gain new skills and knowledge, such as conflict management. And you may want to take the assessment again at the end of the course in about three months to see what progress you've made.

"When I did that several years ago, I found that my scores for relationship management had improved, and I was more confident with the areas that had been flagged as areas for growth on my original report, such as conflict management. Seeing that progress was fulfilling and showed me that I could grow in skills that made my interactions with others less stressful and more fulfilling.

"And guess what?" the professor asked. "The new report identified a different dimension (in my case, social awareness) and three different items where I had room for growth. So I've continued the process of developing my EI skills, little by little, one step at a time. Hopefully you will too. This is how a growth mindset relates to becoming our best self as a leader. There's always room for improvement," said the professor as she ended that day's session.

Reflection:
Emotions Matter

Sam sees that emotions in the workplace are normal because people are both rational and emotional beings. Sam's professor shares a framework that breaks down the complex topic of emotional intelligence into four easy-to-understand quadrants, differentiated by a focus on self and others and divided into awareness and action.

The skills of emotional intelligence include self-awareness, self-management, social awareness, and relationship management, and each area is made up of skills and behaviors that help an individual to function at their best and to be at their best in interactions with others. Sam and the other members of her class learn that each of us has opportunity to grow in one or more areas of emotional intelligence; in fact, refining and enhancing these skills is likely for most people to be a life-long endeavor.

Be sure to complete the quick self-assessment that appears in the next section before you continue reading. Additional suggestions about EI assessments appear in the chapter resources that follow our short survey.

Emotional Intelligence (EI): Quick Self-Assessment

Instructions: Using the following scale, rate as objectively as possible how well you typically display each behavior. Before responding, try to think of situations in which you have had the opportunity to use the ability (but don't labor too long over your answers). Answer with regard to how you *actually* behaved rather than how you *wish* you behaved.

Very Slight Ability		Moderate Ability		Very Strong Ability
1	2	3	4	5

_____ 1. Recognize and express the emotions you're feeling.

_____ 2. Show flexibility in dealing with changing circumstances.

_____ 3. Demonstrate empathy and understanding of others' feelings.

_____ 4. Share persuasive messages when communicating with others.

_____ 5. Identify your strengths and limitations.

_____ 6. Demonstrate self-control of emotions and impulses.

_____ 7. Anticipate, recognize, and meet the needs of others.

_____ 8. Effectively influence others' choices and actions.

_____ 9. Reflect on your past experiences and learn from them.

_____ 10. Show persistence in pursuing and achieving goals.

_____ 11. Support growth and development in others.

_____ 12. Negotiate and manage conflict with or between others.

_____ 13. Display a reasonable level of self-confidence.

_____ 14. Take ownership of your behavior and personal performance.

_____ 15. Perceive a group's emotional climate and power relationships.

_____ 16. Work collaboratively with others in a team context.

Scoring: Enter your answer to each of the questions in the corresponding space.

1. _____	2. _____	3. _____	4. _____
5. _____	6. _____	7. _____	8. _____
9. _____	10. _____	11. _____	12. _____
13. _____	14. _____	15. _____	16. _____

Subtotals _____ _____ _____ _____

Self-Awareness *Self-Management* *Social Awareness* *Relationship Management*

Self-Awareness _____
Self-Management _____
Social Awareness _____
Relationship Management _____
TOTAL EI SCORE _____

Interpretation: This short survey provides some indication of your emotional intelligence (EI).

- If you received a ***total score*** of **65 or more,** you would be considered a person with **high EI**, an asset for leadership and influence with others.

- A score from **32 to 64** is **moderate** and means you have a solid foundation of EI on which to develop your leadership and influence capabilities.

- A score of **31 or below** is **low** and indicates that you realize your EI skills need improvement in order to enhance your leadership and influence with others.

- For **each of the four components** of EI (self-awareness, self-management, social awareness, and relationship management), a score of **16 or above** would be considered **high**, a score **between 9 and 15** would be **moderate**, and a score of **8 or below** would be considered **low**.

Questions for Personal Reflection and Group Discussion

1. This chapter introduced the notion of emotional intelligence and its four major components as a tool for leadership and professional development. Among the four dimensions of self-awareness, self-management, social awareness, and relationship management, which would you consider to be your strongest area? In which area(s) do you believe you have the most room for growth and development?

2. If you haven't already, Ben highly recommends getting the book *Emotional Intelligence 2.0* by Travis Bradberry and Jean Greaves. This book is valuable both for the link to the online emotional intelligence assessment (including a free retest if you want to assess change over time) and for the very practical tips given for developing each of the component skill sets of emotional intelligence. (Please note: The authors of this book don't receive any benefit from recommending the *Emotional Intelligence 2.0* book or the assessment. The authors of that book have been gracious in allowing us to reference their materials and include some of their ideas in this book.)

3. From your own results to our Quick Self-Assessment of EI (or your Emotional Intelligence Appraisal® results from *Emotional Intelligence 2.0*), what did you think about your results? What surprised you the most?

What do you want to do next to better understand and apply the skills of emotional intelligence?

4. The skills of emotional intelligence are often developed best in the context of a specific need, opportunity, or challenge you're facing. What current opportunities do you have for better applying EI skills? Which components of EI will be most important in your situation? Narrow your focus as you start looking for additional resources to support your development.

7

Discover Your Cornerstone in Emotional Intelligence

Sam was glad to be meeting today one-on-one with Lou as her coach. As usual, she had a lot of questions about the leadership concepts she was learning in her MBA coursework and in the Next Gen program and how they applied in her everyday work as a leader.

"Hi, Sam, how are you today?" Lou greeted Sam when he saw her in the company cafeteria where they typically met.

"I'm doing well, Lou," Sam replied.

"I'll bet you have some questions for me," Lou offered with a slight smile.

"Well, of course I do," Sam said, returning the smile. "I want to know how to put to work what we're learning about strengths, emotional intelligence, and leadership. I feel like using these ideas together could make a big difference in how I interact with my team and the results we produce."

"It could, absolutely," Lou replied. "So what questions do you have?"

Sam started to explain, "I want to understand how my strengths and emotional intelligence connect to each other. I learned about talents and strengths in our leadership development class, and we spent a lot of time in the MBA team leadership class looking at emotional intelligence and its components. They've been separate topics, but they're both important to leadership, and it seems to me there must be some connection."

Lou was listening intently and nodding.

"My strength assessment tells me the areas in which I have natural talent. Emotional intelligence sounds like something that you either have or you don't, kind of like IQ. But we have also talked about improving those skills. So I'm a little confused about that, and how my strengths might relate to my emotional intelligence."

"These are important questions," Lou noted, "and I can see how the topics of strengths and EI might seem separate and distinct, while I agree with you that they are really intertwined and support each other. You're right about the fact that most strength assessments reveal areas of talent, meaning a naturally recurring pattern of thought, feeling, or behavior that can be productively applied. Talents become strengths when you add knowledge, skills, and practice and refine your talent to near-perfect, repeatable performance. Notice that the definition of talent includes feelings, which is an indication that talent includes skills in the emotional as well as rational arena.

"As we've discussed in our sessions," Lou continued, "talents have their roots in personality theory. You've seen that talents cluster in four realms of thinking, doing/organizing, relating, and persuading. (Gallup labels these as strategic thinking, executing, relationship building, and influencing. Other strength assessments use different words but have similar groupings.) These four clusters or talent realms correspond with four of the factors in what's known as the Big Five model of personality—five factors that include the dozens of dimensions of personality that have been measured."

Lou mentioned to Sam to review the class handout that contains these bullet points:

- Thinking talents correlate with intellectual curiosity/ openness to experience.

- Doing and organizing talents correspond to conscientiousness.

- Relating talents correlate with the personality factor of agreeableness.

- Persuading talents line up with extraversion (particularly the trait of assertiveness or dominance, the tendency to take charge).

"You've also heard that there's one factor from the Big Five that doesn't correlate with these four talent realms, and that's emotional stability (labeled on some personality instruments as neuroticism, or the absence of emotional stability)."

"Wow, this is a lot to take in," Sam admitted.

"I know," Lou said. "Like the other Big Five factors, we know that emotional stability lines up with some important outcomes including the propensity to become a leader and one's effectiveness as a leader in most situations. Since emotional stability isn't directly reflected in the talent themes, I believe this trait reflects an important, additional dimension that every leader needs in order to deal with personal emotions, challenging relationships, and difficult circumstances in order to apply their talents in different situations. And that's the link to emotional intelligence." Lou paused to make sure Sam was following.

"Sam, you might also be interested to know that the last few years of research on personality point to a general factor of personality or GFP. The GFP includes elements of all of the Big Five factors and is interpreted to be a measure of social effectiveness.

"The GFP also has strong correlations with measures of trait emotional intelligence, or one's tendency to respond to situations and people in socially acceptable ways. Several studies have concluded that GFP and trait EI are virtually synonymous. So there's some real science behind the idea of emotional intelligence as a trait that is a distinct aspect of one's personality.

"Before we explore the link between strengths and EI further, tell me what you've learned about emotional intelligence in your team leadership class," Lou asked Sam, although he knew the answer from his own experience teaching as an adjunct professor in the MBA program at Lantana U. This would be an opportunity for Sam to review and refresh herself on what she had learned and would allow Lou to see if there were any areas where she wasn't confident in her understanding about EI.

Sam summarized what she had learned in class about the emotional intelligence model. "We learned that EI considers the perspective of both self and others. I have to first recognize emotions in myself before I can perceive what might be happening with others' emotions. And both perspectives of EI have two levels—awareness and action (or management). Awareness comes first, then action follows. Four components of EI result: self-awareness, self-management, social awareness, and relationship management. As I'm aware of my own emotions, I can manage my emotional response to be more productive. As I recognize emotions in others, I can manage relationships to support others in a positive outcome from their emotional response."

"Excellent!" Lou exclaimed, proud as always with this coaching client and her ability to grasp concepts and understand how to apply them. Her insight into the four components and how they relate to each other would make this discussion more straightforward.

"The first thing I would say is that your talent themes, because of their link to personality traits, will indicate a propensity for one or more of the components of EI. So, Sam, think of it as your *cornerstone* in EI. In my experience, this has to do with which of the four talent realms is dominant for you. For example, people with doing/organizing talent themes tend to have high conscientiousness and often show a focus on self-management. Even if they're not highly attuned to emotions in themselves and others, they can often work through emotional situations with self-discipline and structure. They're able to manage themselves around their emotions, even if they don't fully understand them, in order to keep going and accomplish their goals.

"But let's talk about another example," Lou went on. "Where do you think people with thinking talents might be oriented with respect to EI?"

"Well, I know thinking corresponds to the personality factor of openness to experience or intellectual curiosity, which includes a tendency for thoughtful reflection. I know I'm fairly strong at self-reflection and learning from my mistakes, so I think it might be self-awareness," Sam offered tentatively.

"That's right!" Lou replied, not surprised that Sam was quick to see the connections. "Again, having thinking talents doesn't necessarily mean someone is well-attuned on an emotional level, but it does indicate they have the skills to analyze a situation, and they are often reflective people, which is key to self-awareness.

"Let's try another one. What would you think about relating talents? How might they align with the skills of EI?" Lou asked Sam.

"The themes in relating seem to align with empathy and understanding others, which would be social awareness, the ability to perceive emotions in others and be empathetic to what's happening with them." Sam paused to hear Lou's reaction.

"Yes, that's exactly the case. Relating talents align with agreeableness as a personality factor, indicating a tendency to be attuned to emotions in others and focused on achieving harmony. Now, what do you think about the persuading talents?" Lou invited Sam's response.

"I'll take a wild guess and say persuading lines up with relationship management, because it's the only component left," Sam laughed and continued. "I know these themes are oriented toward interactions with others and specifically aim to get a response from people. That seems consistent with extraversion as a personality trait and with the EI skills of relationship management."

"Yes, that's a key connection to personality theory, and you would have seen that even if I had asked first about this domain," Lou said. "Persuading talents tend to use communication and influence skills, which often come more naturally to people who have high extraversion, especially the trait within this factor known as assertiveness. I know from our past conversations that you aim to use your talent for communication to align your team, influence your peers, and have an impact on your boss. Talents in this domain are often useful in the EI relationship management skills of communication, influence, conflict management, and so on."

Sam nodded in agreement.

"It's important to remember that the talent domains are simply indicators of an orientation toward one or more of the components of EI. Just like talents need to be refined to become strengths, so this cornerstone skill set for EI may need to be developed and applied," Lou concluded. He outlined the four components on a piece of paper and showed Sam.

Emotional Intelligence Skills, *Talent Realms,* & Personality Factors	Self	Others
Awareness	**Self-Awareness** *Thinking* Intellectual Curiosity	**Social Awareness** *Relating* Agreeableness
Management	**Self-Management** *Doing/Organizing* Conscientiousness	**Relationship Management** *Persuading* Extraversion/ Assertiveness

Alignment of the Four Components of EI with Talents and Personality

"Yes, I can see that," Sam agreed, "but it does seem like those areas would be easier and more natural to develop because of the alignment."

"That's exactly right," Lou said, "so it's an appropriate place to start when a person is trying to understand and develop their emotional intelligence skills."

"In your case, Sam," Lou continued, "we know you lead with a couple of relating talents."

Sam picked up the discussion without skipping a beat. "So that would mean social awareness will likely be my cornerstone," she said and circled that box on the grid.

"That's my strongest and most natural area of emotional intelligence, according to the alignment you suggested. That actually matches with my scores on the emotional intelligence assessment. Social awareness was my highest score, although I know I have room for improvement in all areas of EI, including that one."

Lou responded, "It won't always be the case for everyone that their highest score on an EI assessment matches the area of their talent themes, because we're talking about raw talent, not refined strength. I'm glad to see it aligns so well for you, and it adds what we call face validity to what we're talking about here. For some people, current circumstances and past challenges may have directed a person toward developing other EI skills to respond to the needs they faced. And we know there are those who haven't really even considered the impact of emotions on behavior and may need to grow knowledge and skills in all areas of EI. Knowing your dominant talent domain and how that reflects key personality factors and aligns with the four skills of EI is the best place to start when you're working to assess and improve your EI skills," Lou concluded.

"For me that means starting from social awareness, using my relating talents." Sam paused and reflected.

Lou nodded and affirmed Sam's idea, "Yes, it means recognizing and acknowledging the talents you have among the themes of relating that help you with social awareness, which is perceiving and understanding the emotions of others, showing empathy, and being able to diagnose the emotional needs in situations you encounter with others."

"I believe I do that pretty well," Sam said, almost questioning.

"Yes," Lou agreed, "your scores on the EI assessment support that as your strong suit in EI, and feedback from others likely confirms that."

"People have told me they appreciate how I recognize and address emotions they're feeling when members of the team are going through tough challenges, individually or as a group," Sam confirmed and told this story.

"One of my team members, Olivia, had a child who was undergoing tests for medical problems. Doctors just couldn't figure out what was going on. Clearly, she was so distracted at work, it was hard for her to focus on our rollout of the new customer service initiative. I noticed it. I called her in to offer some support from the company's Employee Assistance Program. I also assured her that I understood her concerns and that family comes first. We agreed she would take some time off under the Family Medical Leave Act so she could better focus on her child's needs."

"That's an excellent example," Lou said. "The opportunity, as with any talent, is to recognize it and build upon it, to be more conscious and intentional in developing a talent into a strength that can be used in a variety of situations.

"But let me ask you this, Sam, are there situations where you think you've been less effective in identifying and addressing emotions, in showing empathy to others?"

"I think—" Sam started tentatively and then continued, knowing she would have Lou's understanding and support in exploring this opportunity, "when things are really busy and we're working hard toward a deadline such as a project milestone or completion, I sometimes don't pay attention to the stress and emotion the team is feeling. In some cases, we accomplish our goal, but people are burned out and a little resentful of the way I pushed them to get there. It's ironic, because that's the same behavior I reacted to strongly when I felt my previous director was pushing me to get results more quickly and not understanding any of the obstacles I faced. I resented it and felt it put more distance into our working relationship."

"In these situations, would you say that you don't sense the stress and emotion, or you sense it and don't respond to it?" Lou asked, helping Sam to consider further what she just said.

"I think in some cases I sense it but don't realize how strong the feelings are, or I just want to power through the situation and get to the goal," Sam said. "I sometimes don't realize how the stress and emotions have affected me, and especially how they have affected others, until we're done with the project and able to look back."

"That seems like a key insight for you," Lou noted, "and it may indicate a need to enhance your self-awareness in these situations as well. We can come back to that idea, unless you want to explore it more right now." Lou paused to check with Sam on where she wanted to go with this conversation.

"It's fine with me to move on for now. We can come back to where I may need to build my self-awareness or other EI skills. I want to understand how I can better use my social awareness in that kind of situation, because it doesn't serve the team well when I just expect everyone to push through the stress. I can even think of a couple of cases when I ignored the warning signs and one or more people on my team had an emotional meltdown before we completed our work. This resulted in delays as well as hurt feelings and frustration," Sam said.

She considered her next thought. "In one case I'm pretty sure I lost a team member because I was pushing too hard. After one particularly stressful project, she got upset with me, and we had a couple of tough conversations. She left for another opportunity a month or two after that incident."

"Looking back and remembering that example, what would you do differently in that type of situation in the future?" Lou asked.

"I think first of all I would pay *more* attention, not less, when the team is going through a challenging time with lots of demands and deadlines. Powering through the situation to try to get to the goal hasn't always led to the best results. So I need to make sure I'm paying attention to emotions and stress."

"You said you're often aware, at some level, of what the team is feeling. How could you handle that differently?" Lou asked.

"I think I need to make it part of my checklist as I'm looking at how we're doing as a team relative to deadline and demands we're facing. I'm able to figure out the best path to get us to the goal most efficiently, but I tend to gloss over the emotional needs of the team in those situations."

"And what would that look like?" Lou asked, pressing gently for more specifics.

"Well, I think it means that I build something like emotional stamina of the team into my review of projects and workload, and I make it an agenda item for the team when we meet to discuss our progress. Those are often short, stand-up meetings to check in quickly with the team on where they are and what they need, but we could take another minute or two to assess where we are in our emotional capacity and stamina to complete a project."

"How do you think the team would respond to that?" Lou asked.

"They would have to know that I'm sincere in asking," Sam acknowledged, "so I would have to be consistent with asking and convey that I really want to know how they're doing."

"How could you best convey your sincere interest?" Lou asked. He kept pushing.

"Literally stopping for a moment, taking a deep breath, asking a question like, 'How are you doing with everything we're trying to do right now?' and pausing for answers from each member of the team. And when someone identifies a need or expresses a frustration, I need to respond to it in some way, not just nod my head and go back to work on the project."

"Those are some key points," Lou agreed. "You said you want to respond in some way, so what might be some options in that moment?"

"Sometimes acknowledging the feeling and agreeing with the frustration go a long way to people feeling heard and understood," Sam said. "In some cases someone may be asking for some flexibility in how they get their part of a project accomplished because a need is bubbling up in some other area of their work or their life. We've all been there, and team members are usually understanding and helpful when that happens."

Sam stopped and took a deep breath. "I remember one time when we were approaching an important deadline and my daughter got sick. She couldn't be in school, and I didn't have anyone else to help care for her at the time. Every parent's dilemma, right? So I had to be home. My team rallied, picked up the slack, and kept me informed of progress as I worked from home for a couple of days. They reached the goal on time, and I know how much I appreciated the support."

"I love that example," Lou said. "It sounds like you've experienced the support of the team in that kind of situation, and I imagine you've been able to provide it to others too."

"Yes, although it sometimes has become a crisis before I did. That's where I want to improve, checking in regularly and paying attention to the early warning signs. And I believe I have some ways to do that now by assessing the needs of the team as I evaluate progress, checking in with the team on how they're doing, and ensuring I make note of what they say and take some action in response."

"Excellent!" Lou said. "That's a nice summary, and a powerful example of how you can be even more effective in social awareness with your team, using your relating talents in a more purposeful and intentional way. This has been an excellent discussion and illustrates well how you can build on your strengths to be even more effective with your core skill in emotional intelligence," Lou said as he checked the time.

"We still have a few minutes left, so let's consider other ways in which the intersection of your strengths and emotional intelligence might be helpful."

Reflection:
Dig Deeper into EI

Sam learns about the connections among the four skill sets of EI, four of the Big Five personality factors, and the four realms of talents and strengths. This helps explain how some areas of EI may come more easily for a person than other areas.

In Sam's case, this involved her dominant strength realm of relating, supported by high agreeableness on the Big Five and confirmed by her relatively high score in EI social awareness. This is her cornerstone among the EI skills. Her candid self-appraisal, guided by her coach, also revealed skills for growth and development in several areas of emotional intelligence, including additional skills in social awareness, her cornerstone.

Sam comes to understand the need to center herself in emotional situations and to ensure she is showing empathy and compassion for what others are experiencing even when she might be coping well.

A sample assessment of emotional intelligence was provided at the end of chapter 6. We now recommend that you compare those results with the sample strength assessment that you did in chapter 5. Which EI skill was rated highest? What was your dominant realm in terms of your strengths? What similarities and distinctions do you see between your strengths and your EI skills? How can these insights help you to be a better leader?

Questions for Personal Reflection and Group Discussion

1. This chapter addressed the alignment of the four realms of strengths with the four components of emotional intelligence. How do your strength assessment results line up with your emotional intelligence results? What do your results, and specifically your dominant realm (or realms), say about possible foundational skills in EI?

2. If you had more than one realm tied for first place, with a couple of strengths in each, which of those realms seems to come more naturally for you? Or are both about equal?

3. Sam found there were stressful situations where she had difficulty applying even her dominant realm of strengths. How has this looked for you? What are the situations (or people) that tend to put you off-balance in applying your strengths as you typically would?

8

Expand Your Toolkit for Emotional Intelligence

After talking about Sam's natural tendency toward social awareness coming from her relating strengths, Lou shifted the coaching conversation with her to consider other areas for development within emotional intelligence.

"Sam, we've discussed how each of us has a cornerstone in emotional intelligence that aligns with the main area of our talents and strengths, but obviously each of us should be looking to improve in all of the skills across the four areas of emotional intelligence: self-awareness, self-management, social awareness, and relationship management."

Sam nodded. "It's reassuring and empowering to realize I already have strengths that equip me for at least one of the four areas of EI, and I can see the benefit of growing in all four areas. But how do I do that?"

"As with any new skill, you do it one step at a time. It will be important to focus on a particular skill and identify specific behaviors that you want to develop and strengthen. And it's usually best to do that in the context of a specific situation or challenge you're facing. We'll explore that in just a moment."

Lou reached into his briefcase and pulled out a chart. As he pointed to the elements on the graphic, he said, "The second principle of strengths-based emotional intelligence that will guide you on the path of developing other areas of EI is simple and straightforward. Let me just emphasize that **you can use *any* strengths (across any of the four realms of thinking, doing, relating, and persuading) to develop new skills in any area of EI.**"

Strength-Based Toolkit for EI
Any Strength Can Be Productively Applied to *Any* Skill

Thinking	Doing/ Organizing	Relating	Persuading

Self-Awareness	*Social Awareness*
Self-Management	*Relationship Management*

Strengths Applied to Emotional Intelligence

"Wow, that's a very broad statement!" Sam said with a look of surprise.

"Yes, it is," Lou replied. "Especially since we had a narrow focus with a person's primary area of strength, showing how their dominant domain of talent aligns with a specific area of EI. With this second principle, we broaden our focus to show that any strength can be applied to any area of EI that you're trying to develop. The idea is that you use the strengths you have to accomplish the things that you need to do.

"In their book titled *Strengths Based Leadership*, Tom Rath and Barry Conchie showed how any of the thirty-four talent themes could be used to address the most important needs of every team—to build trust, show compassion, provide stability, and create hope. Likewise, I believe if you're trying to develop any new skill or behavior, especially in the area of emotional intelligence, you can apply any of your strength themes," Lou said.

"That's an interesting idea," Sam said, "and it certainly gives me hope that I can grow further in the skills of emotional intelligence, regardless of what strengths I'm starting from."

"To see how this applies, let's talk through an example that would be helpful for you," Lou suggested. "Is there a specific situation in your work right now where you believe applying your strengths and enhancing some aspect of emotional intelligence might make a difference?"

"Yes," Sam replied without hesitation. "Yes, there is. The analyst who supports my team really pushes my hot buttons. His name is Mike. He's a smart analyst but tends to keep to himself, and he's a little cynical about the company. He doesn't participate in many of our team activities, and I've heard that he makes light of me behind my back with other team members for the things I do to celebrate success with my team. I've tried to pull him in more to team meetings and celebrations, but he always makes an excuse to not participate."

"It sounds like he may have hurt your feelings a little bit by making light of what you do with your team," Lou noted.

Sam paused and reflected. "Yes, but it's more than that. I really need Mike to be aligned with the rest of the team and to bring us data and information that is helpful to improving what we do, not just what he thinks we need or what the system already gives us."

"What would be your goal for working with Mike?" Lou asked.

"I'd like him to participate more in team meetings and learn more about what the reps do in gathering information to settle claims. I'd like him to design reports that help the reps focus on the most critical information that will help them do their jobs better and more efficiently."

"That sounds like a tall order but really important to your team's performance and improvement," Lou noted, and Sam nodded in agreement. "Now remember, as we've discussed before in coaching, your goal must be something you can do, not anything that's dependent on Mike changing. Otherwise it's just wishful thinking."

"I guess I'd say that I want to figure out some ways to be more effective in drawing Mike into team meetings and events, and encourage and reward his engagement with the rest of the team. Ultimately I'd like to hear from others that he's helping them do their jobs better," Sam said.

"Okay, that sounds more focused on what you might do in your interactions with Mike, as his manager, with some validation of results from others on the team. Which aspects of emotional intelligence would help with this challenge?" Lou asked.

"I guess we're in the realm of relationship management, especially the skills of influence and leadership."

"Anything else?" Lou asked as Sam paused thoughtfully for a moment.

"Well, I can see how all of the EI skills could contribute to success here. I need to stay self-aware of the reactions I'm having with some of Mike's behavior that keeps me and others at arm's length. I need to manage my emotions when he pushes my hot buttons and I feel frustrated that he's not responding as I would like him to. And I suppose I need to ensure I'm empathizing with his point of view about the situation, so that I can manage our relationship more effectively," Sam said.

"Those are excellent insights," Lou noted, "showing how all of the EI skills work together in a situation to make us more or less effective. Where would you like to start in order to address this challenge?"

"I do want to think about my self-awareness and self-management as I'm interacting with Mike, and to ensure I'm using my social awareness in a way that's understanding of his temperament and personality, but I'd like to use this time to come up with some strategies I could use to influence him more effectively."

"Then I'm going to give you some homework," Lou said with a smile, "to write in your leadership journal how self-awareness and self-management come into play in your work with Mike, since you already acknowledged that he can push your hot buttons. We can talk about that in our next meeting.

"Let's focus today on your interactions with Mike and how you might influence him more effectively. But I'm going to suggest that we first look at your social awareness. We know that awareness precedes action in the EI framework. Overall, this is an area of strength for you, but you acknowledged that you're experiencing some challenges in applying your social awareness to someone like Mike."

"Yes, that's true," Sam replied.

"You mentioned Mike's unique personality and temperament. Of course, every person is unique—one of a kind, we might say. But what are some of the attributes you see in Mike that are different from other members of your team?" Lou asked Sam.

"Certainly, his level of interaction with others is different," Sam offered, reflectively. "Most of my team is extraverted and interactive throughout the day. It helps them to get work done, share ideas, and occasionally blow off a little steam when they have a difficult interaction with a customer or get frustrated with a tough challenge.

"Mike doesn't engage with the rest of the team in much of that interaction. He works in his cubicle with earphones throughout the day. When he takes breaks, he goes off by himself or maybe goes to lunch, usually with one of his analyst friends. When he has a question, he'll come to me or go and ask another member of the team. I've noticed if others join the conversation, he fades into the background and just listens, then eventually wanders off and goes back to his cube."

"It sounds like he's a pretty strong introvert," Lou observed. "He prefers interaction one-on-one with people he knows, and he fades into the background as more people join in the conversation."

"Yes, that's true," Sam replied, "so how do I encourage him to interact more with the entire team? He could learn a lot from others."

"If I might offer an observation," Lou paused, and Sam nodded, "that sounds like how you would view the situation, and I really hear your extraversion and persuading talents in that question. Let me encourage you to also bring in your sense of empathy and your relating strengths into this situation. How do you think Mike is viewing his interaction with the team?"

"Oh, clearly he prefers talking one-on-one with me or other team members," Sam noted. "We can be very interactive as a group sometimes," she said with a smile. "The pace of conversation increases, with lots of ideas flying around, and we can get a little loud trying to break into the conversation."

"That's probably a little overwhelming to him, like sensory overload," Lou interjected.

"Yes, that's a good term for it. I've seen him on multiple occasions walk away from the whirlwind of one of our team discussions, then come back later and ask someone what was decided."

"Who does he approach on those occasions?" Lou asked.

"Sometimes he comes to me," Sam said, "or if I'm not available, he will often talk to Sara. She is one of the most experienced employees, and Mike and Sara worked together in another group before each of them came to my team a few months apart."

"It sounds like they have a strong rapport," Lou noted. "How could you capitalize on that relationship to help Mike be more effective in supporting your team?"

"I suppose I could have requests for new reports go through Sara, since they work together so well," Sam suggested. "And maybe encourage them to meet every week or two to discuss trends the team is seeing and if any new information would be helpful."

"These ideas should be helpful to the situation, and you're certainly being respectful of Mike's preference for one-on-one interaction," Lou said. "And notice that we've shifted from social awareness to relationship management as we talk about actions to improve the situation with Mike. Having him interact more with a team member who already has a strong relationship with him is a good start. Now let's talk about your interaction with Mike and how you can make it more effective for both of you. If it's been frustrating for you, chances are it is for him too."

"I hadn't thought about that before, but I can see what you're saying," Sam admitted. "We've been in this tug-of-war between different styles, and I'm sure that's no easier for him than it has been for me."

"At some point you may want to say that to Mike," Lou noted, "so he knows you're aiming to do some things differently. He's more likely to see the difference in your approach if you tell him that you realize communication may have been difficult and you want to change the way you approach your interactions."

"I can do that," Sam said. "I want him to know I'm trying, and maybe that will also help him to see opportunities for new ways to interact with our team. I suppose I could even ask him about his preferences for communication with me and the rest of the team. I don't think I've done that."

"That sounds like a superb idea that would demonstrate your empathy and your interest in his communication style and preferences," Lou said. "Then you'll want to listen to what he says and work together to put some new ideas into practice."

"Lou, you're right, I don't have to have all of the answers ahead of time, do I?" Sam asked, as much to herself as to Lou. "That would show I really care about his point of view too. So taking a different approach to managing the relationship really is an extension of focusing on my relating talents first, isn't it?"

"Yes, I think you're onto something there," Lou replied, "and it shows how you might build on something that already is a strength, or maybe it's applying a strength you already have in a fresh or new way. You also said you want to influence Mike more effectively. Which of your strengths do you think you could apply to do that?"

"I suppose I'd want to use my persuading talents, such as my communication strengths, but in a way that's not overwhelming to him," Sam said.

Lou nodded and said, "You've already noted how empathy could be applied in this situation to better understand his communication preferences as a more introverted and analytical person. I believe you might also consider how other relating talents could be used in this situation."

"What do you mean?" Sam asked.

Lou continued, "Relationships can be built in many ways. Some people don't know any strangers. They're constantly making new friends and maintaining a broad social network. Other people tend to prefer a few deep friendships to having many acquaintances."

"That's definitely more the pattern for me," Sam acknowledged. "I can get along well with most people, but I only have a few people in my life that are truly my friends and confidants."

"That pattern for a few in-depth relationships tells me that you're able to establish trust and build a sincere relationship with people that goes beyond day-to-day work interactions. For example, you've talked about how you know personal details about your team members like their family members and their hobbies and outside activities."

"That's certainly true," Sam said thoughtfully. "So with Mike, I could use my relating talents to build a stronger one-on-one relationship with him rather than constantly trying to bring him into group activities. That seems to fit his style and preferences better, don't you think?"

"Yes, I think you'd be using your same strengths with a different emphasis," Lou said, confirming Sam's idea. "Instead of your relating talents being amplified by your strength in persuading to touch more people, you could apply your relating talents by focusing on the individual relationship and building trust, better communication, and ultimately influence with Mike."

"That makes a lot of sense," Sam replied. "I think with Mike I need to put the emphasis on building a strong one-on-one relationship rather than trying to pull him into the group's activities.

"It also occurs to me that I can use my persuading talents in a different way. I tend to use a strong and confident communication style, which works well in a group setting. With Mike, though, I need to apply listening in equal measure to speaking so I make sure we're having real dialogue with equal contributions."

"I believe that's a key insight," Lou said with enthusiasm. "It will feel a lot different than the high-energy back-and-forth discussions you have with your team. But listening is hard work too."

"Yes, I remember we talked about that in our training. It's easy to hear someone but takes work to listen, right?" Sam asked.

"It does," Lou agreed. "Most of us are equipped to hear what someone is saying, but how often do we really feel listened to?"

"Not very often," Sam noted, "and I imagine Mike feels that too."

"Excellent point, and there's one final thought I have for you to consider in this situation, if you're open to another idea," Lou offered.

"The more ideas the better, in this situation!" Sam exclaimed and leaned forward.

"I'd encourage you to also consider your talents in doing and organizing. High achievers like you typically get a lot of satisfaction from accomplishing goals, and not just by yourself but working with others to achieve a goal."

"Yes, you're right about that," Sam said. "That's certainly how I feel when I work with the people on my team to finish a project or achieve our monthly goals. The shift from personal accomplishment to working with and through others was a big shift when I went from individual contributor to manager. Now I find the team's accomplishments more fulfilling than anything I achieved on my own."

"I believe that's the potential in you working with Mike in some of the new ways we've discussed," Lou concluded. "You will build a stronger relationship, have more influence, and accomplish more together."

"I'm excited to get started," Sam said with a smile. "This situation is definitely an opportunity for me to apply several talents in slightly different ways to be more effective with one individual in our work context. And I can see your point that any strength can be applied to improve any area of emotional intelligence as I work with others."

"You're welcome, Sam, but the ideas are yours, and of course you'll have to try out some new behaviors and possibly make some adjustments to achieve the results you hope to achieve in working with Mike. I look forward to hearing about how it goes for you," Lou said as they gathered their paperwork and coats as the lunch crowd started pouring into the company cafeteria.

Reflection:
Challenges Matter

In this chapter we saw Sam realize how to apply her talents in multiple areas (relating, persuading, and doing) to enhance her relationship with Mike and potentially to become more persuasive with him. These examples illustrate the idea that a person can take any of their strengths to apply to new goals and challenges.

Sam also saw ways to use her strengths in slightly different ways that would better fit the needs of one of her employees. Making these adjustments will show compassion to people and commitment to the larger goals that the team is working to fulfill. This idea foreshadows how EI skills can actually enhance the use of one's strengths, as we'll see in the next chapter.

Take a moment to reflect on your own strengths and emotional intelligence. Have you had people in your life (like Mike was for Sam) who presented a challenge to you? How did you apply talents or fail to apply talents? Can you see that you did or could have either emphasized or downplayed one of your strengths in order to improve the situation? It is our emotional intelligence that tells us how and when to dial up or dial down a strength as we face challenging situations—a topic we'll explore further in the next chapter.

Questions for Personal Reflection and Group Discussion

1. What is a current challenge or opportunity you're facing in your job or career? What areas of emotional intelligence might need extra emphasis in order to address this challenge or fulfill the opportunity?

2. Which of your core talents or strengths might you employ to enhance the areas of EI that need to be expanded? Remember, these strengths don't necessarily have to align with the dimension of EI you're addressing. You can use *any* strength to address *any* area of EI. Also, strengths in combination with one another are often the powerful combination needed when you're building new skills.

3. If you're not part of a group discussing these questions, consider talking with a coach about how to best address your challenge or opportunity. And remember a coach might be a professional business coach, a peer familiar with you and your situation, your current manager, or other leaders in your organization willing to take the time to support you in your development.

9

Deploy Your Strengths with Good Emotional Intelligence

It was the monthly meeting of the team leadership class, and Lou was standing at the front of the room beaming like a proud parent as Sam told the story of how she had applied her strengths to interact in some new and different ways with one of her employees, which he knew, as her coach, was about her recent success working with Mike.

"Thank you, Sam," Lou said as Sam concluded her story. "That's an excellent example of how someone can use talents from multiple areas to tackle a challenging situation. You had frustrations with the relationship with your team member and applied strengths in persuading, doing, and relating to improve the relationship. We've heard some similar examples from several others today of the same idea, and I'm glad to see how each of you has applied your strengths in some new and different ways to increase your emotional intelligence skills.

"Now there's one more principle we want to discuss today as we wrap up our discussion about strengths and emotional intelligence," Lou explained. "We've already seen two big ideas. The first is that your dominant realm of strengths shows your cornerstone skill set with regard to EI. Going back to the example we just heard from Sam, we know her primary talents were in the relating area. So from the standpoint of EI, she has an innate tendency for social awareness. This quadrant of the EI skills grid is her foundation and home base, so to speak, with respect to emotional intelligence.

"The second big idea, then, is that you can apply any talent in your toolkit to improve any aspect of emotional intelligence where you want or need to improve. Again, I'll go back to Sam's example. She wanted to expand relationship management skills to more effectively influence a member of her team. Sam used her persuading talents (related to her strength in communication), her empathy and relating talents, and her doing/organizing talents (being a high achiever, eager to work with others to accomplish goals) in some new ways. She changed how she communicated with this team member, and the result has been a more productive and fulfilling relationship for both of them."

Lou stopped there so the group could absorb the two big ideas. He noticed many opening laptops to take notes.

"In these two ways," he went on, "both your cornerstone in EI (based on your dominant strength realm) and your toolkit (that is, all of your strength themes) will help you develop the skills of emotional intelligence.

"The third big idea turns the focus back the other way, from EI to strengths. Enhanced EI skills will enable you to use your strengths more productively. Specifically, having strong EI will help ensure you don't overuse or misapply your strengths, and help you know when to apply or even amplify a particular strength."

Lou waited a moment as everyone turned that idea over in their heads a time or two. And Manuel spoke up.

"So, let me get this right. Strengths can help enhance my emotional intelligence, and emotional intelligence can enhance my strengths?" he asked somewhat tentatively.

"Yes, there are benefits in both directions," Lou said, endorsing part of what Manuel had said, and then clarified. "EI doesn't necessarily *enhance* our strengths but can help us utilize them more appropriately in different situations and with different people, which in the end makes them more effective."

Lou continued, "When you have well-developed EI skills—and those are self-awareness, self-management, social awareness, and relationship management—they enable you to regulate the application of your strengths in different social situations and interpersonal relationships. There is emerging evidence that the relationship between strengths and performance is curvilinear, like an inverted U shape. Greater use of strengths leads to higher levels of performance, up to a point. Then the curve flattens and turns downward. Using a strength too much, or using it in the wrong context, results in a decline in performance.

"I'll use myself as an example," Lou said. "My top talent in the persuading realm is related to continuous improvement, maximizing opportunities, and taking what is and making it better. For me this strength is always 'on' as I scan situations, myself, and other people and find opportunities to improve things. Improvement or making things better is the motive that drives much of what I do. Unregulated, I've found that can drive people a little crazy at times. Who wants to be around someone who always thinks we could do better instead of just relaxing and helping others to enjoy where we are?" Lou smiled.

He showed the next PowerPoint slide to make his point as the discussion continued.

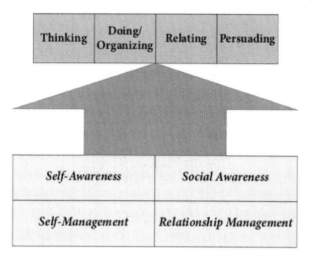

Emotional Intelligence Applied to Strengths

"For example, after this class today," Lou said, "I'll immediately start thinking about how the class went—what went well, but especially what didn't go as well as I would have liked and how we can make it even better in the future. It's as natural to me as breathing.

"When I'm working with other facilitators, like having Jennifer here today for the first half of our session, I need to be careful. If I start talking immediately about all of the opportunities for improvement, Jennifer may walk away thinking, Lou wasn't very happy with the class today. I wonder if he's upset with me? Now I know Jennifer isn't really going to be bothered by any feedback I provide about today's class, because she shares the desire I have to make it better," Lou said with a nod toward his cofacilitator.

"But a new member of the team, or someone who brings a different focus such as ensuring the smooth execution of the class, might take offense with my immediate critique of the class and how it can be improved. They might wonder, What was wrong with that? I thought the class went well, or Why is Lou being so critical? Trust me, I've had conversations like these with people in the past, and I have received feedback that I have sometimes come across as cold and lacking compassion, that I'm too focused on the task at hand and not enough on the people involved in doing the task with me."

Based on her coaching conversations with Lou, Sam was not surprised to hear him being so candid, and she hoped others appreciated his transparency as much as she did.

"So I've learned (through increased self-awareness)," Lou said as he pointed to the box on the graphic as he explained each one, "to hold my thoughts about improvement (self-management) for when they will be best received by others (relationship management) based on my understanding of those with whom I'm working (social awareness). In some cases, that simply means taking a few minutes to celebrate success and talking about what went well in the class before I share my ideas for making it better.

"In other cases, it might mean writing down my thoughts, ensuring I have a balance of plus and minus comments and do a more formal review. In many situations, I need to be sure and ask others for their ideas first, because they may have seen some of the same things I did, and even things I didn't see. They will be a lot more committed to making changes if they've helped to identify the opportunities than if I just announce what needs to be done," Lou said.

"I still share my ideas. Don't get me wrong. It's almost like I'm compelled to do so," Lou said with a smile, "but I regulate how and when I do so, based on applying EI to the situation, taking into account timing, and making careful consideration of others and how they might receive my ideas."

Sam spoke up next. "I think that's part of what I was doing with my team member when I changed the way I communicated with him. I was trying to force him into the same style of communication that I prefer, which as you all know by now is very verbal, interactive give-and-take, and that works well with most of my team members but was overwhelming to him."

Sam saw heads nodding as she continued, "Through a coaching conversation with Lou, I came to see how I needed to first apply my relating strengths to my interactions with this team member and adjust the way I used my communication strength from the persuading realm in order to best influence him. I also found a connecting point with him around a shared talent from the doing realm, which is setting and achieving challenging goals."

"Sam, that's a perfect example of this principle in action, and the results you reported about improvements in the relationship are striking, and quite impressive to someone like me who wants to *maximize every opportunity*," Lou acknowledged with extra emphasis, and the rest of the class laughed as they heard the connection Lou made to his own strengths.

"Does this just mean we're using our signature strengths less?" Raj asked. "You said we want to be careful not to overuse or misapply them."

"That's true in the sense we want to use our strengths in a way that's appropriate to the situation and the people with whom we're interacting," Lou replied. "I often refer to EI as the regulator on the application of our strengths. To some extent, it means seeing our strengths through the eyes of others and making sure they don't overwhelm or put others off.

"But a regulator is also used to speed up or increase intensity of whatever it's regulating—in this case our strengths," Lou continued. "EI can help us recognize when the situation is right for bringing our strengths with more intensity, and when they will not only be received well by others but actually appreciated in conjunction with the strengths they have."

"I think I might have an example of that from a recent crisis my team experienced," Sam began. Lou nodded, encouraging her to continue. He wasn't sure which example Sam might share, but he was confident that her comments would be on point to the discussion.

Sam said, "A couple of months ago, our CRM (that's the customer relations management) application crashed in the middle of the day. For those of you who don't know, a CRM is a tool like a highly developed spreadsheet that allows you to track current and potential customers. The members of my team use this app all day, every day to look up history and document the conversations they're having with our customers.

"I came back from a meeting and everyone seemed to be just sitting there, looking stunned. Silence had replaced the usual buzz of phone conversations and background chatter when members of the team would discuss issues they had heard from customers and how they solved them. It was very unusual to see everyone so quiet and clearly frustrated," Sam said, as she turned in her seat to speak more directly to the group.

"I knew intuitively that it was a situation where my communication talents were needed for persuading the team to address the problem. I immediately gathered the team around and we started talking about the situation and what we could do to address it. I had to calmly yet quickly draw them into the discussion. We didn't know how long it would be until the app came back online. In the meantime, phones were ringing, going to voice-mail or being placed on hold, and the backlog was growing by the minute." The frustration of the situation was showing in her voice.

"After just a few minutes of discussing the challenges and some alternative solutions, the team decided to get back on the phones and take notes in a word processing document. These notes would need to be uploaded into the CRM system later, but it would be a simple copy-and-paste operation.

"It also meant that my team members wouldn't have access to the scripts and guidelines in the CRM to address different situations, and this was a big concern to the newer team members who relied on those guides and notes. Someone suggested a triage system where anyone who wasn't familiar with an issue could place a customer on hold and ask for help from a more experienced member of the team. They discussed how the handoffs would be done, and within minutes everyone was back on the phones, interacting with customers, and doing their jobs. And the buzz of conversations, on and off the phones, was back and stronger than ever!"

"That level of communication must have sounded wonderful to a communicator like you," Lou noted with a big smile.

"It did, of course," Sam agreed, "but everyone told me later how much it helped that I got the discussion started after the app crashed. The team actually came up with most of the solutions. And it turned out that even the newest members of the team needed to refer very few calls to a more experienced team member. The newer members of the team realized they didn't need the scripts as much as they thought. The crash actually became a big confidence builder for several of them, but they appreciated having the safety net of the triage system."

"What follow-up did you do?" Raj asked.

"When the CRM app came back online late in the day, I huddled with the team again and we took about ten minutes to talk through a plan to update records with the notes they took offline. Several of my team members needed to leave work on time because of family commitments, picking up their children or going to after-school activities. The team agreed those people should start putting in their updates while others covered the phones. I authorized overtime pay for the remaining team members to get caught up after normal work hours concluded and the phones were quiet. By the end of the day, just ninety minutes beyond our normal hours, everything was caught up," Sam reported.

"That's a perfect story," Lou said, "as an example of when your persuading talents were needed even more than usual, and you used your emotional intelligence to dial it up, so to speak. Your team obviously responded well, and everyone benefited from you doing what you love to do."

"I didn't even realize what I was doing until a couple of people pointed it out at the end of the day," Sam said. "They said they appreciated how I got the team talking and addressing the problem instead of just sitting there feeling frustrated and waiting for the app to be fixed."

"That's an excellent example for all of us as we wrap up this module on the benefits of emotional intelligence in how we deploy our strengths," Lou concluded.

Reflection:
Ensuring Strengths Don't Become Weaknesses

Sam and her cohorts learn that not only can strengths be used to enhance one's emotional intelligence, but enhanced EI skills enable a better deployment of one's strengths. This includes avoiding misapplication or overuse of one's strengths *and* encouraging focused application of strengths in situations that call for more.

You might do this intuitively already, as in Sam's example of working with her team during a particularly stressful set of circumstances. How much would your leadership and team results be enhanced by dialing up strengths more intentionally and purposefully in your work and interactions with others?

In this chapter we also got some insight from Lou. He shared that he can overuse his desire to improve situations, so much so that it gets in the way of his social awareness. It is almost as though he becomes overconfident in his strengths.

As Lou shared, he has learned—through social awareness and relationship management—to use his maximizing strength in more judicious and compassionate ways. Are there any strengths you have that you could dial down? What about others on your team? How would you go about making changes?

Questions for Personal Reflection and Group Discussion

1. What examples can you see in your past behavior when your emotional intelligence helped you to know when to dial down a particular strength in a situation or interaction? Remember (and preferably write down) the factors that created awareness that you needed to use your strengths in a different way. By understanding how this has worked for you in the past, you can build on success in situations you will encounter in the future.

2. What examples can you see in your past behavior when your emotional intelligence helped you to know when to dial up a particular strength in a situation or interaction? Again, write down these factors that brought awareness of an opportunity to use one or more of your strengths more in that situation. This understanding can also help you build on success in future situations and interactions.

3. In situations when you've gotten feedback indicating that your strengths came on too strong for some people, what have you learned? Have you modified your behavior (if so, how)? Do you communicate to others how you plan to employ your strengths in challenging situations? (This may prepare them for your unique approach, and it can also bring about broader conversations about strengths within a team.)

10

Build Your Resilience

"Today's class marks the halfway point for your cohort in the Next Gen Leadership program," Lou began as he opened the class session. "And it's unique because we're not going to summarize a bunch of research or just give you another framework to apply for success. Instead, we're going to tap into the collective wisdom of this group of leaders in your cohort and let *you* tell *us* what you've learned about a very important topic."

Sam looked around at the group she'd become familiar with, some even friends, and she was eager for this session. Lou had hinted she might be surprised.

"Our focus today is resilience, which is made up of two factors. First, the ability to bounce back from problems, challenges, and setbacks in your work and even more broadly in your career. Second, the ability and willingness to learn from those previous challenges. It is not just about bouncing back, there is also forward momentum and growth. Resilience is enhanced through emotional intelligence skills and the application of your strengths to the biggest challenges you have faced," Lou said.

"Our format is a series of interviews by the three of us who are your facilitators. Each of us will interview one of the members of this cohort for whom we have served as a coach. Through your sharing, we often find vivid examples about past success in spite of overwhelming obstacles. Of course, we bring these examples to you with the full cooperation and consent of your colleagues with whom each of us will be speaking. Not everyone chooses to be this vulnerable to come in front of a group of their peers and share their most difficult situations. That's okay. We're grateful for the courage of three of our students who have agreed to share their stories with you.

"I'd like to begin by interviewing Ms. Sam Denton. Please welcome Sam to the spotlight." Sam's colleagues gave a loud round of applause and shout-outs as she joined Lou at the front of the room. She was glad she wore her favorite suit to work that day.

"Welcome, Sam, and thanks again for being willing to share your story with us today," Lou said.

"If others can learn from my experience, I'm happy to share my struggles and what I've learned," Sam said as she and Lou settled into their chairs.

"Remind us, Sam, you've been a manager at ATA for how long now?" Lou asked.

"I've been a manager for two years, but my initial experience was very difficult," Sam began. "As recently as a year ago, I wasn't sure I wanted to be a manager any more, and I was considering leaving the company."

Several people gasped and had looks of surprise on their faces when Sam said this because she was such an enthusiastic member of their cohort.

"I think we all have those moments in our career when we wonder what we've gotten ourselves into," Lou interjected.

"Yes, that was the case with me," Sam agreed. "I remember thinking this isn't what I thought I was signing up for when I became a manager. I wanted to manage others because I thought I could help others grow and develop and be successful in their careers."

"That's a key motivation for becoming a manager," Lou noted, "and of course being responsible for the performance and the development of others is a major responsibility in the job description of a manager. So how was the reality different from your expectation?"

Sam decided to go for it. No reason to hold back here in this safe group. "A couple of factors played into my shock and disillusionment. I became the manager of a team that was one of the lowest performing in the division and had been for a while. The first surprise was that some people seemed to have given up on their work, the team, and the company. They didn't seem interested in growing and improving, and after several bad experiences with managers in the past, they weren't inclined to trust me to make a difference."

She tugged her jacket together and continued. "The second thing was that I assumed I would have some time to establish relationships, build trust, and help people develop skills and knowledge to improve their performance. I believe that process takes time, but there was an expectation that I would turn things around quickly, maybe because the team had been doing poorly for a while.

"My director at that time (not the one I have now) put a lot of pressure on me to get results quickly. I fell into the trap of thinking I could do it because I had the best intentions and was enthusiastic about making a difference. But the team didn't know me, didn't yet trust me, and weren't ready to make changes. I really needed some mentoring that I did not get."

"How did this make you feel?" Lou asked.

"It was very frustrating, of course," Sam said, and she felt even now the stress of those early days with her team. "It really shook my confidence when people didn't respond to what I was doing. And the pressure from my director made me feel like I was the problem, that someone else would be able to do this with no issues. The fact was, others had tried before, and everyone had dug into their respective trenches for the battles that would follow."

When she looked around the room, she saw friendly faces and felt comfortable sharing her story.

"What bothers me most looking back is that I allowed the situation to throw me off-center from who I was, and who I wanted to be as a leader. People were pushing me for results, and I started pushing the team. I knew they were frustrated but so was I!" She saw heads nodding.

"Instead of showing care and compassion for the team and the situation they were in, I fell into the pattern they had seen again and again. I was pushing hard for results and not accepting any excuses. The situation was complicated by the fact that the company went through some downsizing that year and I had to remove three members of the team when the positions were taken away."

"Even under the best of circumstances, that can shake up a team a lot, I would imagine," Lou noted.

"Yes," Sam agreed, "even though I removed those who were the lowest performers, and in a couple of cases the people who were also the most negative about the team and the company, the rest of the team was on edge about what might happen next. It played right into the drama they had experienced with previous managers. At a time that we should have been pulling together, the team was falling apart, and there was no sense of community or support."

"So your team is going through this stressful time with the rest of the company," Lou summarized, "and I would imagine your stress was compounded even more because of the feeling that this wasn't what you expected it would be like to be a manager."

"Well, yes, umm, you said that very nicely," Sam hesitated, "but to be blunt, I was feeling a little sorry for myself. I was also worrying, feeling burned out, and had trouble sleeping." Several students nodded their heads as if understanding her feelings.

"I decided I wanted to get through this difficult time as quickly as possible, so my next step," Sam said, "with approval from my director, was to put three more people on a performance improvement plan for ninety days. Whew! I actually believed at least a couple of those people could make the changes needed, but you can imagine how that felt to them coming right on the heels of the downsizing."

"They might have felt like you were out to get them," Lou offered.

"Exactly! And at least one of them told me that to my face. I couldn't convince them that I really wanted to help them turn their performance around. One left within a month for another opportunity, and the other two hung on to the end of the performance improvement plan with little or no change, getting more and more negative over the next ninety days. And of course, their negativity affected the rest of the team, including me." Sam paused to take a sip from her water bottle she had placed next to her chair. She let out a deep breath and continued.

"I think many people assumed they would be the next to go, and we would ultimately disband the entire team. And there were days when I was convinced in my own mind that I would be the next to go. I was having very difficult conversations with my director on a weekly basis, sometimes daily."

"So, we see a team—and a leader—in crisis, at a time that was tough for a lot of people in the company, but circumstances had really compounded to make the situation worse for your team," Lou summarized.

"That's right," Sam agreed. "I knew we weren't alone, but it sure felt lonely. I had become a manager for the first time, but I felt like there wasn't anyone I could safely talk to about what I was experiencing and what the team was dealing with. Of course, there was no time to go to training courses like this or connect with peers in other ways, so I felt very isolated."

"What finally made a difference for you and your team?" Lou asked.

"I'd like to say that I had this flash of brilliance and turned things around overnight," Sam smiled, "but that's not how it happened.

"As awful as it felt, and as poorly as I think I implemented it, removing some of the lowest performers and particularly those with the most negative attitudes was the beginning of a turn of events. I was still able to fill the positions that were vacated by those on performance improvement plans. I was very deliberate and intentional in the hiring process to fill those positions. I also included other team members in the screening process so everyone had a voice in who joined the team. I felt like it was the first positive thing I was able to do as a manager.

"I got a new director about this same time. I don't really have anything bad to say about my previous director. I believe the pressure I was feeling to turn things around quickly was just a reflection of the pressure he felt from others above him. But the new director came with a very openly stated goal of engaging, supporting, and developing people. This was truly a breath of fresh air after the strong focus we'd had on results at any cost." Sam paused to take a breath. Was she revealing too much, she wondered.

"While he acknowledged that our group was still one of the lowest performing, my new director said he would give me some time to improve our performance, and he involved me in discussions about how to do that. This allowed me to recenter around the values that attracted me to be a manager in the first place. Our conversations about how to make needed changes started to build my confidence rather than tear it down. I felt more committed as we expanded our team back to full strength and brought in some people with fresh perspectives and more positive attitudes."

"That sounds like quite a turnaround for you," Lou said.

"Yes, Lou, but it wasn't just me. I believe the whole team could feel the difference. I felt compassion for the team that I hadn't felt in a while, and team members started supporting each other rather than just worrying about themselves. We began to build a sense of community." At this point in telling her story, the group could see that Sam's demeanor noticeably softened, almost as if to tear up.

"And I've heard members of my team talk to others in the division about everything we went through and that we actually came out stronger on the other side. I felt genuine gratitude for my team. To me, that's the greatest measure of success," Sam concluded.

"And a true indication of resilience," Lou affirmed. "Coming out stronger on the other side, as you said. I like that!"

At this point there was a spontaneous round of applause from the class. Several class members thanked Sam for sharing her story.

"I know we're all glad to hear that the situation has turned around, Sam, for you and your team," Lou said, "and I could just leave your story right where we are as a lesson for all of us to benefit from." But Lou continued as he transitioned into the lesson of the interview. Sam returned to her regular seat and opened her laptop to take notes.

"But I also believe this is a teachable moment, and I want to highlight that your story illustrates the principles that author and consultant Joel Bennett and colleagues have called the Five Cs of Resilience. This is the framework we're using in our class for this important topic.

"Consider what Sam talked about in each of these five areas." Lou introduced a PowerPoint slide with five bullet points as he summarized the Five Cs of Resilience:

- **Centering**. "Sam, notice that you actually used the term *recenter* when you shared your story. Your well-being (such as worry and lack of sleep) had been upset. However, the support you got from the new manager allowed you to recenter. You maintained a certain poise and calm by returning to the values, skills, and strengths that drew you to being a manager in the first place. The team returned to taking care of each other and not just worrying about themselves. Centering is about returning to self-care, to values, and to finding ways to remain calm as a habit. This way, when the going gets rough, we come back to some internal compass. For a team, the opposite of centering would be constant drama and conflict and a focus on different opinions and polarizing discussions rather than finding time for relaxed connection."

- **Confidence**. "Sam, your confidence was shaken but then grew when you felt you had time to make a difference and a director who was supportive of what you were doing. Confidence also equates with a key concept of self-efficacy in self-leadership. Self-efficacy is a belief in and positive attitude toward our own abilities, especially our ability to meet challenges and achieve our goals. Everything we have talked about in this class has been geared toward helping you build your confidence. Sam, it's very encouraging to see how your own confidence has grown from the challenge you faced and also has grown throughout this program."

- **Commitment**. "You reaffirmed your commitment to being a leader to your team and to the organization through this challenging situation. Commitment means perseverance, a stick-to-it-iveness, a sense of purpose, dedication, and follow-through. At all levels of resilience—in a person, a team, and organization— it is often commitment that helps us get through even the most adverse situations."

- **Compassion**. "You and your entire team showed concern for each other as you started to rebuild. You may remember from a previous class how I shared that sometimes my need to improve everything gets in the way of my being compassionate. Over the years, I have learned that compassion can be expressed in many ways—like being generous, friendly, supportive, and encouraging. We also need to be compassionate with ourselves and not be too hard on ourselves."

- **Community**. "Your description changed from a group of employees to a team and a community of people who support one another. This reinforces the point that resilience is rarely achieved alone. We always benefit from a strong social support network. I like to think that our class has become a community over the life of this course. There is open discussion, cooperation, fellowship, and working together toward a common goal. I think I heard all of those in your story, Sam. Interestingly, community is often the most vivid aspect of resilience we see after a major crisis. After a hurricane or earthquake people rally together to help each other. That was certainly the case after the tragedy of 9/11."

Sam commented to Lou and the group, "Those Five Cs make an excellent framework to understand resilience, and I appreciate the connections you made between those points and my story. I mentioned that at times I felt very lonely. Much of what changed had to happen inside of me, yet I know I never would have made it without the support of others, including my director and all the members of my current team. I especially like that the Five Cs occur inside of us but also in the team."

Resilience

Resilience is the ability to not only bounce back from stress and adversity but also the ability to transform the stress experience into a learning experience and, hence, provides a basis for thriving in the future. For many, resilience entails significant adversity and even trauma. Resilient leaders are those who have faced and overcome failures and, through that experience, are better able to serve and bring out the strengths of their teams. Following the writings of coauthor Joel Bennett (author of *Raw Coping Power*), resilience contains five qualities that reside within individuals and teams, the Five Cs: centering, confidence, commitment, compassion, and community. These qualities may also be strengths.

"Lou, all of this overlaps with other ideas we've learned. I would also go back to what you said at the beginning of this session. Because of the complex challenges I had to deal with, I also grew more in the skills I now know to be part of emotional intelligence such as self-awareness, self-management (including motivation), social awareness/empathy, and relationship management."

"I appreciate the connections you made, Sam," Lou said. "In fact, by sharing your story with all of us, it also felt authentic.

Again, compassion also includes self-compassion. And when you combine that with poise and sticking to your values, you have real authenticity. Remember your self-assessment of strengths? This also fits with your tendency to lead from the heart."

Sam said, "Thank you. I don't believe I made any progress in resolving the challenges or building resilience until I returned to a focus on my strengths and my values. I wouldn't have necessarily described it that way at the time, but that's what happened. In one sense I came to the *end* of myself with burnout, worry, and despair because the situation got so bad. I was literally ready to throw up my hands and walk away. Yet part of what eventually transformed me and my team was coming back to the traits that make me unique in my approach as a leader and how I work with others, and those are the specific strengths I use and the values that guide me."

"Thank you, Sam," Lou said as he led another round of applause for Sam and her story of resilience.

At this point, Lou reached behind the desk to pull out a bag. He passed the bag around and asked each student to reach in and pull out only one of the many envelopes. Students then opened each to find differently colored and beautifully designed cards. Each of them had some saying about resilience.

Jamal read his: "'You have power over your mind, not outside events. Realize this and you will find strength,' from Marcus Aurelius."

Caitlyn exclaimed, "This is great. Mine is a quote from Helen Keller: 'Character cannot be developed in ease and quiet. Only through experience of trial and suffering can the soul be strengthened, ambition inspired, and success achieved.'"

"I love that," Sam said. "It sort of summarizes everything from this class, doesn't it? It makes me think—this whole course is also about building character. Here is mine: 'She stood in the storm, and when the wind did not blow her way, she adjusted her sails,' from Elizabeth Edwards."

Character and Values

Character (as in "a person of character"). Character "applies to the aggregate of moral qualities by which a person is judged apart from intelligence, competence, or special talents," if you examine a dictionary definition. In other words, a person can have qualities of virtue, goodness, moral soundness, integrity, and authenticity as aspects that are independent of talent or the ability to perform. We use character in *Your Best Self at Work* because, for some individuals, their best self may be due more to their overall moral character than to strengths, skills, or talents.

Values. Put simply, a value is a standard or principle that one considers worthwhile or worth pursuing or upholding in word, behavior, and lifestyle. Very often, our best self at work emerges when we decide what is most important and meaningful and then behave in ways that align with those values.

Reflection:
Adversity Builds Character

What motivated Sam's willingness to share? What are the risks in her sharing? What are the benefits? Sam's story illustrated the Five Cs of Resilience, a framework formulated by one of the coauthors of this book, Joel Bennett and colleagues (in early research on team resilience and his book, *Raw Coping Power: From Stress to Thriving*) and validated by research. Thinking back through previous chapters, which of the Five Cs do you think has been the most important for Sam's growth?

Our ability and willingness to share our resilience story is the first exercise in *Raw Coping Power*. Get out a journal and write your own story and, if you find the right person, you can take turns sharing about how you recovered from challenge. For now, consider where you are with respect to the Five Cs today.

When you've struggled with stress, overwhelm, or burnout, which factors have been missing in your life? How has each component of the model contributed to your resilience in the past as you came through difficult challenges? How have your strengths and emotional intelligence—your character—come about because of challenges and adversity in your own life? Also, please complete and reflect upon the Five Cs that follow. What connections do you see between your strengths and these Cs?

Resilience—Quick Self-Assessment: The Five Cs of Resilience

There are three steps to this exercise:

First, rate your level of agreement with each of the following statements. The boldface items are more specific to a workplace setting.

1 = Strongly Disagree
2 = Disagree
3 = Neither Agree nor Disagree
4 = Agree
5 = Strongly Agree

Centering	Rating
I have healthy coping skills that give me perspective on life.	
I know how to slow down and take a break when I need to.	
My coworkers and I work at an even pace, not rushed to deadlines.	
I am more likely to pause and take a breath rather than react strongly if someone says something that irritates or angers me.	
Subtotal for **Centering**	

Confidence	
People I know would consider me competent and self-assured.	
I can handle most problems that come my way.	
People at work believe that their work is important.	
Faith and inner strength have helped me get through difficult times.	
Subtotal for **Confidence**	

Commitment	
When difficulties arise, I persist in solving things rather than giving up easily.	
My life has been a story where I have pursued the dreams and values that are important to me.	
My coworkers and I can accomplish what we set our minds to.	
I am a loyal and dedicated person in at least one area in my life (in such roles as a spouse, parent, religious participant, or employee).	
Subtotal for **Commitment**	

Compassion	
I recall a time recently where I helped someone who was going through a hardship or life problem.	
It is easy for me to feel pain or upset when someone I care about has similar feelings.	
People at work show concern when problems happen in our families or wider community.	
People I know consider me a kind, generous, or sympathetic person.	
Subtotal for **Compassion**	

Community	
There is at least one person in my life whom I can tell my troubles to.	
I have others who care for and support me.	
People at work communicate well with each other.	
During stressful times, I spend at least some time getting support from others rather than withdrawing and trying to "go it alone."	
Subtotal for **Community**	

Overall Total (Add the 5 Subtotals together)	

What's most important in this assessment is your own interpretation of the results. Which of your scores were highest? Lowest? What surprised you? Consider how much you identified or resonated with each of the twenty phrases. Is there one C that stands out to you more than others? Which combination of phrases is most important to you?

Some guidelines to consider: The range of Total Scores on this assessment is 20 to 100. Scores of **80 and above** indicate a **strong** level of resilience. Consider how you might share with others the resilience practices that have helped you, and how you might support others who are struggling in this area.

Total Scores of **50 or less** indicate **room for growth**; consider reading and using the tools in Joel Bennett's book, *Raw Coping Power*, and other resources on resilience.

Total scores **between 51 and 79** would be **average**, and you might benefit from development of one or more of the Five Cs. If any of your Subtotals are 10 or less, you could benefit from some work in that area.

Second, review the five **bolded** phrases that are in the set of twenty statements. Note that these phrases refer to resilience in your **team or work group**. As you reflect on these five workplace or team-related statements, reflect on the following questions:

- Which of the Five Cs is strongest in your team or among your coworkers?

- For each of the Five Cs, who among your coworkers is the "best" or strongest at it?

- If you were to ask your coworkers, what would they say about the Five Cs in you? Which of the Five Cs would they suggest *you* are strongest in?

- Which of the Five Cs needs the most development in your team? In you?

Consider sharing this resilience survey with your coworkers and ask them to complete it. Then, get together to have a discussion. During that discussion, use your strengths and emotional intelligence skills to guide the discussion. Use this exercise to bring out the best self at work in yourself and others.

Third, meditate on each of the Five C areas in the following diagram and come up with your own word or phrase for each. You can use any word(s) you wish, whether or not it is shown in the boxed diagram. Following these exercises, ask yourself, what does resilience really mean to me? Journal whatever answer comes forth. Place sticky notes with key terms on your mirror, bulletin board, or other location where you'll see them often.

relaxed focused takin' a break
present inward coping reflecting
"breathe easy" meditate calm
concentrate self-care acceptance

Centering

vacation **solitude** MANAGING tranquil
unwind slow down *settle back*
decompress ease **prayer** revitalized
'take it easy' hang loose recline
calm down refreshed "chillin"

caring help generous **grace**
supportive reaching out kindness
BENEVOLENT lending a hand
sympathy friendly humanitarian

Compassion

hug **generous** NUDGE ALONG forgive
hospitality assist *SELFLESS* befriend
kind-hearted comforting **charity**
goodness empathy accommodate
loving encourage tender-hearted

goal-oriented PLANFUL achieving
problem-solving forward-thinking deliberate
PERSEVERE dedicated follow the dream
promise-keeper diligent decisive

Commitment

sense of purpose handshake invested
responsible loyal *DEVOTED* mission
CALLING **follow-through**
deliver sworn carry out "take oath"
persist **Vow** clear direction EMPOWERED

COMPETENT effective **hopeful**
optimistic hardiness positive focus
FAITH courageous knowledgeable BOLD
assured willing assertive reliable

Confidence

determined confronting *TOUGH*
certainty firmness *FEARLESS* fierce
re-assuring nerve **backbone**
brave audacious "look in the face"
adventurous gutsy lion-hearted

support meeting discussion
neighborhood area village commune
kinship unity identity spirit
cooperation team convergence

Community

solidarity gathering "US" age-group
ethnic-group network *Social Media*
commonwealth club **family**
coming together "work it out"
fellowship union commons

(Adapted from Bennett, J. (2014). *Raw Coping Power: From Stress to Thriving.* Published by Organizational Wellness & Learning Systems, Ft. Worth, Texas. ISBN 9780991510207.)

Questions for Personal Reflection and Group Discussion

1. When you think about the idea of resilience, how does it reflect your unique talents and strengths? What similarities do you see?

2. Resilience also operates at the team level. What do you believe is the best combination of the Five Cs for any team or work group that you are currently working with? Is there someone in the group who exemplifies or illustrates one of the Cs best? What can you do to acknowledge and enhance all of the Cs among your team?

3. How has emotional intelligence fueled or supported resilience for you in the past? Consider two or three specific examples.

4. How has the combination of strengths and emotional intelligence helped you to be resilient in challenging circumstances or relationships?

11

Plan for Continuing Professional Development

Sam could hardly believe that her first term in the MBA program at Lantana University was almost complete as she came into the classroom for the final session. It had been a whirlwind of learning—reading, discussions, papers, and a team project that had helped her and others in the class see the application of what they were studying.

Tonight, the class was discussing an article about professional development and turning in a final part of their Leadership Portfolio. The first assignment for the portfolio had been a report on their emotional intelligence scores and other assessments, which led to a learning plan for the semester. There were multiple journal assignments along the way. This final assignment focused on the development plan they wanted to pursue after the class.

"Are you giving us homework after the semester ends?" one student had asked Dr. Marybeth Lambert with his best imitation of a whining voice, knowing by now there had to be a reason for this assignment that went beyond their class.

"Yes, I am," Dr. Marybeth said assertively, then added with her trademark smile, "because your development as a leader should always be continuing. You will retain from this class only those habits that you put into practice. And one of those ideas is that you should never stop growing as a leader. You should always have goals for new learning and putting into practice what you've learned." She opened the PowerPoint file and clicked the first slide.

"As you see in the Individual Development Plan template we provide for the class, you should give attention to both strengths and areas for development. In the optimal situation, those two areas will be linked. That is, you'll be applying one or more of your strengths to build a skill or implement a new behavior that is going to help you be more effective," she explained.

"Your development goals may be tied to your emotional intelligence appraisal or other assessments you've completed in our class, or it may be a skill or behavior identified through feedback from others. It's usually helpful if you can tie this to a specific situation, challenge, or opportunity at work."

By now, everyone in the MBA class had begun taking notes about the ongoing assignment, including Sam.

"For example, let's say you've identified the need to improve your skills in managing conflict based on results in the relationship management area of the emotional intelligence assessment," the professor explained. "This was confirmed by feedback you've received in the past from others, noting that you tend to avoid or smooth over conflict rather than deal with conflict more directly and resolve your differences with others. You see this skill as being important because you've been asked to lead a project with a team that has some strong personalities, including one person with whom you've had conflict in the past. You now have a clear focus and strong motivation to develop new skills and behaviors in conflict management.

"For your strength to leverage, the components of the plan are simple and straightforward, since this should be a theme which you have productively applied in the past," and Dr. Marybeth clicked the PowerPoint slide to show the points:

- Name the strength.

- Describe how you identified it as a strength—from a talent or strength assessment and/or feedback from others.

- List three specific ways you will apply that strength in the current situation.

"This last part may require some reflection as you build the plan for your development goals. This section of the plan is more detailed since you are working on new skills and behaviors that you haven't necessarily used before, or you may be applying them in new ways. The key components here include these bullet points," Dr. Marybeth said. She moved to the next slide:

- State each development goal in specific behavioral terms.

- Give the reason for the goal; remembering why you set a particular goal can help maintain your motivation as you're learning and applying new behaviors.

- List at least three specific action steps for each goal. These should be observable behaviors that will demonstrate the skill you're aiming to develop. If it's an EI skill, your Emotional Intelligence 2.0 report will provide ideas on action steps. You may want to also look for other resources, including talking with others who may have ideas or reflecting on the Five Cs of Resilience.

- Each action should have a start and end date. While you will continue using the behavior beyond that date, this range provides a time period for focused practice, reflection, and seeking feedback on your new behavior and its impact on yourself and others.

- Next, consider potential obstacles that might get in the way of your new skills and behavior. This might include time constraints, resistance from others, and your own tendencies against change.

- For each obstacle, describe your plan for overcoming that obstacle. For example, if you list *time* as a potential barrier, consider when you will work on learning and practicing your new skill and how you will hold yourself accountable (or seek accountability from others).

The professor picked up the lesson: "When you get to the end of the time period for your goals and action steps, you should revisit and update your development plan. This should be done at least every six months, to keep your professional development plan relevant, alive, and evolving to the changing needs of the workplace."

Dr. Marybeth concluded, "There may be many activities you do in the future to continue your development. I'm suggesting classes, coaching, reading, and talking with colleagues and friends. The development plan is simply a way to keep focus and momentum as you continue to grow as an effective leader."

Reflection:
Development Planning

Personal and professional development always extends beyond a single class or growth experience we may complete. Sam and her classmates learn the value of having an ongoing Individual Development Plan that is frequently updated. Using a planning template will build upon key psychological principles such as the value of specific, measurable goals, leveraging one's own strengths, EI, resilience, and motivation for change, breaking down daily action steps, incorporating realistic time frames for change, and anticipating and addressing potential obstacles.

You should give attention to at least one strength to leverage in addition to areas for growth and improvement. What items are (or should be) on your development plan?

Part 1: Strength to Leverage

Name Your Strength:	Basis for calling this a strength: (Feedback from others, strength assessment, etc.)

List at least three ways you can maximize this strength and/or use it as leverage to develop other areas of effectiveness as a leader:

- _____

- _____

- _____

Part 2: Individual Development Goals

Development Goal 1:	Reason for This Goal:	
Specific Action Steps:	Start Date:	End Date:
Potential Obstacle(s):	Plan to Overcome Obstacle:	

Development Goal 2:	Reason for This Goal:	
Specific Action Steps:	Start Date:	End Date:
Potential Obstacle(s):	Plan to Overcome Obstacle:	

Individual Development Plan Template

Questions for Personal Reflection and Group Discussion

1. How does your current organization use professional development plans? Is it part of the performance management process? Have you had discussions with your manager or others about areas where you want to grow and develop?

2. If you don't already have a professional development plan, use the template in this chapter to start one (also available as a PDF file on our website, YourBestSelfAtWork.org). As suggested in the template, include at least one strength to leverage and two skills or behaviors you want to develop or improve. Of course, it's even better if the strength(s) on your plan line up with the areas you want to develop.

3. Share your development plan with your current manager and with one or more coworkers who can help hold you accountable and support you in the development process. Update your plan regularly (at least once a year) as circumstances change and as you accomplish your goals and see new opportunities for growth.

12

Summary and Next Steps

Sam was excited but a little sad as she met with Lou today. Excited, because she knew she would walk away with some new ideas through her dialogue with Lou, and sad because it was the last scheduled coaching session as part of their leadership development class.

After reviewing her latest efforts relative to the coaching goals she had set with Lou at the beginning of the process, Sam asked, "Now where do we go from here? I know the formal coaching process wraps up with this session, but I still feel like I have so much to learn."

"Continuing to learn is important," Lou noted. "Frankly I'd be a little worried if you thought you had arrived at leadership perfection after this one program. I've been doing this for a long time and continue to learn more about leadership with every class and every coaching session. And working with you has been a pleasure because I know you have the same continuous learning mindset. Actually, a growth mindset."

"Thank you," Sam responded. "I've enjoyed having you as a coach because of the genuine dialogue we've had over some situations that were really perplexing me. I feel like I've made headway in leading my team and working with each member of the team in a more positive way."

"You're welcome," Lou said, acknowledging Sam's gratitude, "although I'll remind you that you were the one who came up with the solutions and followed through with action. I just helped to create an environment for you to reflect on the challenges and to decide for yourself how to apply the lessons you were learning.

"And that leads us to the next step, which is an update of your goals as part of a professional development plan that goes beyond the leadership program you've completed. We're quick to note that the program is just one part of your ongoing journey to grow as a leader."

"I've already done an updated development plan as part of the leadership class in my MBA at Lantana, and here's a copy for you," Sam said with a look of pride as she shared her plan with Lou.

"I definitely want to keep learning," Sam noted, "and teaching others what I've learned so far. I think that helps me to learn some of the principles again and keep them fresh and relevant to what we do."

"Great point," Lou said, "and I'd expect this plan to include not only the areas in which you want to continue to grow and develop but also how you will coach and develop others as a leader.

"So let's review where we've been in the cohort program here at ATA, which I know dovetails nicely with the team leadership course at Lantana. This program focused on a few key concepts—strengths, emotional intelligence and resilience—that allowed us to explore many aspects of leading a team," Lou said.

"First, we focused on understanding your strengths and how that reflects core elements of our personality. Research and experience indicate four main areas where our talents and strengths cluster together:

- Thinking
- Doing/Organizing
- Relating
- Persuading

"We explored your strength assessment as an indicator of core talents, which you will apply in a wide range of situations. *Naming* these talents, *claiming* them as your own, and *aiming* them for greater effectiveness helps ensure the use of your strengths is purposeful and intentional, not random and haphazard.

"Sam, you had a strength theme from your assessment in each of the four realms of talent, and relating was your dominant area, with two themes," Lou said as he personalized the information to his protégé.

"Yes," Sam agreed, "and that dominant area was confirmed by other feedback I've received on the job over the years."

"I'm glad to hear that you were able to get that confirmation from your real-world experience and feedback from others," Lou said.

"We saw that emotional intelligence was made up of four components, based on the perspective of self and others on two levels—awareness and management:

- Self-Awareness
- Self-Management
- Social Awareness
- Relationship Management

"After introducing both topics—EI and strengths— we talked about three big ideas linking the two concepts. The first big idea was that your dominant area of strengths indicates an area of natural talent that provides a *cornerstone* in building emotional intelligence skills. Each talent area tends to indicate relative strength in one of these four quadrants of emotional intelligence:

- Thinking → Self-Awareness
- Doing → Self-Management
- Relating → Social Awareness
- Persuading → Relationship Management

"In your case, Sam, your strength in relating pointed to a natural tendency to have social awareness as your home base or comfort zone within EI."

Sam agreed. "I think that's why I often heard from others that I was able to connect, empathize, and understand what others were feeling from an emotional standpoint. I didn't have the words to describe it before I did a strength assessment, but I can see how my relating talents keep me well-attuned to others' emotions."

"Whereas with other aspects of EI," Lou continued, "you probably have had to be more conscious and intentional in developing the skills and behaviors associated with those areas."

"And that's been true as well." Sam smiled. "I was often so focused on others that I wasn't always consciously aware of my own emotions. I remember us talking about flexibility in an earlier class. I sometimes didn't manage myself well in the context of emotional situations. I was observant of others and empathetic toward them, but I put my own emotions on the back burner. I remember you mentioned that I showed self-compassion when we talked about resilience. That was very helpful to me.

"Also, I could get a little stuck sometimes in an empathetic state yet not knowing what to do next. The EI model showed me there's a difference between *awareness* of others' emotions and *management* of relationships and situations when emotions come into play, just as there is on the self side. Working on relationship management, EI skills helped me to know what to do to positively influence others in the context of emotional situations, while also being kind to myself," Sam said.

Next, Lou said, "The second big idea was that *any strength*, from any of the four talent realms, can be productively applied to grow any of the skills of emotional intelligence. This represents your full *toolkit* for developing EI. A person may have strengths in the realm that corresponds with a particular aspect of EI, but you're not limited to those. The philosophy of strengths-based development is that you use the strengths you have to do whatever you need to do. Each person's strengths combine in a unique interaction that makes you uniquely *you*.

"Sam, you had talents in each of the other domains to apply to each aspect of EI, such as using your drive for achievement (from the doing realm) as a way to set goals and measure progress for yourself in some of the skills of self-management. But you also used skills outside of that one talent realm. For example, I know you applied your thinking talents and love of learning to gather information and find best practices in self-management," Lou said, and paused.

"Yes," Sam nodded, "learning was important for all of the skills I was working to improve. I also used my communication talents, from the persuading realm, to gather ideas from other people who I knew practiced self-management skills. That strength interacts with my learning talent, so all of my learning wasn't from a book or training program; it also came from talking with others."

"That's a nice example of how strengths can work together," Lou agreed and then presented the third point.

"The third big idea was that enhanced emotional intelligence has a reciprocal benefit for our strengths, enabling us to utilize our strengths more appropriately in different situations and with different people based on how we read them. EI can help us to avoid overusing or misapplying a strength, as well as highlighting opportunities when it's appropriate for us to use a strength with more intensity."

"I love that idea and have definitely seen the benefit," Sam exclaimed. "With my communication talents, I sometimes need to dial it back with some people because it may overwhelm them or, in some situations, like when others have the same strength and we start competing for air time."

"Yes," Lou noted, "you did well in regulating that strength also in your interactions with your team member Mike, who preferred one-on-one discussions with you or another team member rather than jumping into some of the bigger team discussions.

"We also talked about the fact that using EI to regulate our strengths doesn't just mean that we have to dial down our strengths. Having strong EI also means we recognize the times, places, and relationships where we can best serve the need of the moment by dialing up a particular strength or set of strengths."

"Yes!" Sam said with enthusiasm, "I had that insight in our last class when I realized that was what I did when my team faced the challenge of fielding customer calls while the CRM app was down. They were feeling down and almost paralyzed by the circumstances. I gently but quickly dialed up my communication talent to get them talking about the challenges and possible solutions, and as a team they successfully overcame that challenge and gained a lot of confidence in their abilities as a result."

Lou nodded and smiled, saying, "That's an excellent example of what happens when we use EI to read the people and circumstances around us and productively bring our strengths forward in all of their fullness to help others. The results are admirable, and the team is also strengthened. When you bring your best self to work, it sets a remarkable example and raises the bar for others to be better and work together better too."

Sam said, "That story also points to what I think is the fourth big idea that I learned from the resilience section. It is through challenges and difficulties that we can learn to tap into and even develop or refine our strengths. By drawing on centering, commitment, confidence, compassion, and community (the Five Cs of Resilience), we can build both our strengths and our emotional intelligence."

A broad smile came over Lou's face. He gave Sam the "two thumbs-up" gesture and said loudly, "That's it! You got it. All of these start to come together, to align, as we walk on the path of leadership development. It is the process of discovery and applying our wisdom. *That* is the hallmark of true leadership!"

Unifying Concepts: Alignment and Best Self

Alignment. Alignment has a particular meaning in *Your Best Self at Work* and refers first to the coordination or finding connections between our strengths and emotional intelligence (EI). While certain strength realms link to specific EI skills, we can use *any* strength to develop any area of EI, and we can use our EI to assess whether we should express ("dial up") or downplay ("dial down") a strength within a particular situation or interaction. We learn to adjust, arrange, and calibrate how we express our strengths and EI in order to bring our best self to work. Alignment also includes integrating strengths, EI, and resilience together. For example, through adversity we become stronger and can also better lead others as we use EI to discern which of our strengths helps us overcome particular challenges.

Best Self. The idea of best self comes from the notion that effective leaders know how to bring out the best in others. This means helping people to be true to their values and facilitating conditions that bring their full set of strengths and express their full talents, skills, and competencies. One's best self may also be expressed through resilience, following adversity. The overall purpose of this book is to help you bring your best self to work.

Reflection:
Looking Back Helps

Sam has the opportunity in this final conversation with her coach to review the many diverse experiences she has had over the preceding months to learn more about leadership effectiveness by exploring the distinctive aspects of her personality, her core talents and strengths, the concepts of emotional intelligence, and how these different elements relate to each other.

Sam renewed her commitment to being a leader and growing as a leader as she applied her strengths and expanded her EI skills. She is on the path of becoming her best self at work, with benefits accruing to all of the relationships in her life as well as her own well-being.

Refer back to the first chapter of the book and the reflection at the end. You were asked to think about which elements of Sam's character might be most important to her growth as a manager. Looking back over all that she has learned (and you have learned), can you discern how your initial assessment was correct? What surprises did you have about her? About yourself? How have each of the three areas—strengths, EI, resilience—played a role in your own growth? How can they as you move forward?

Questions for Personal Reflection and Group Discussion

1. Review the four big ideas of the book about strengths, emotional intelligence, and resilience summarized in this chapter. Which has been the most meaningful for you? How do you see that idea connecting with the others?

2. Which area needs the most attention for you at this stage in your professional development? Consider your own profile of strengths, EI, and the Five Cs of Resilience, as well as your relationships at work and challenging circumstances you may be encountering.

13

Expect the Unexpected: Going through Challenging Times

It had been six months since the Next Gen Leadership program wrapped up, and what seemed like a strong economy was now in a tailspin, not just domestically but around the world. No one knew when life might get back to normal, but everyone agreed the new normal would look different.

Sam's phone had been ringing all morning, and she was about to let the latest call go to voice-mail when she recognized the number.

"Hello, this is Sam," she answered and was glad to hear a familiar voice on the other end of the line.

"Hi, Sam, this is Lou," said the voice on the phone. "I know we're done with the Next Gen program, but I like to check in with my students from previous offerings. With everything that's going on these days, I was looking forward to connecting with you. How are you, Sam?"

"Oh, Lou, as you can imagine, it's been really tough lately." Sam felt an instant rapport with Lou and let her guard down quickly with her coach. "The ripples of the current economic crisis across our country and around the world have affected all of us, even strong companies like ATA. We've had a big slowdown in our business and just finished a round of layoffs that affected almost every part of the company. The changes are accelerating our efforts in process automation, so there's even more work for those of us remaining as we aim to be as efficient as possible."

"Wow, it sounds like a lot has happened, and I'm not surprised," Lou affirmed Sam's rather grim assessment. "As you said, everyone is feeling the effects of the current crisis, and we all know people who have lost their jobs and had big changes in their business. How has your team been affected?"

"At this point, I've only had to furlough one of my team members as the entire company went through a 10 percent budget cut. As you know, that puts everyone on edge, wondering what might happen next, and we're looking for efficiencies everywhere, including restructuring our departments and preparing for the possibility of more job cuts."

"Sam, how are *you* doing with all of the turmoil and uncertainty?" Lou asked.

"That depends a bit on what day you ask me, or even the time of day," Sam admitted. "You know I worked hard to build trust with my team and help each of them be the very best. It's always hard to have to let people go. And I know every position is vulnerable, even my own. But I also know a lot of people who have already lost their jobs, or their companies have closed the doors completely, so I'm grateful to have my job and be in a position to make a difference."

"That makes sense," Lou agreed. "There are a lot of emotions that accompany turmoil like we're experiencing. I hear your sadness and frustration but also optimism and hope that you can make a difference moving forward."

"That's right," Sam stated. "It's a whirlwind of emotions as we try to stay focused and make the best decisions possible in the midst of a lot of uncertainty. And if I'm holding steady through the storm, it's not just because of my own strength. I'm fortunate to have amazing support from the other members of my team, my boss and peers, my husband and family, and other friends and colleagues who are part of my network. These relationships help to sustain and encourage me."

"How has this affected you and your work, Lou?" Sam turned her attention to her coach and mentor. "I know our company has had to suspend many of our professional development programs here as we've reduced our budget."

"Thank you for asking," Lou replied. "Yes, the Next Gen program went on hold after the last cohort finished. But it's not the first time that's happened. I'm fortunate to have work elsewhere, including in some public institutions that haven't had the same downturn, at least not yet. But in many cases new work has gone on hold, and even where I have ongoing coaching contracts, people are too busy right now to meet. But I've also had some work pop up in unexpected places, as some people see this time as an opportunity to retool their credentials or make a change."

"Ah, there's that word again: opportunity!" Sam exclaimed. "That's a dual-edged sword, especially in times like these, isn't it?"

"Yes, I often remind people that the Chinese word for crisis includes the characters signifying danger and opportunity," Lou noted. "Some people have the fight/flight/freeze response from the danger, and others may feel the same emotions but then move quickly to take advantage of new opportunities."

"Yes, that's interesting," Sam noted, "because we do hear in some essential industries that companies are actually hiring and staffing up because of the crisis. I know in the past I've had recruiters contact me frequently. Lately the number of calls has decreased, but they certainly haven't stopped. One recruiter has been very persistent in calling me about an opening that he maintains is a real opportunity for someone with my experience. How can I know if I should stay where I am or launch off to something new?"

"Well, there's no easy answer to that question," Lou responded, "and you know as a coach I wouldn't tell you what you should do anyway. You ultimately have to answer that question for yourself, just as I've had to do in past situations. You're obviously well regarded at ATA as a graduate of the Next Gen Leadership program, but no one, including me, can give you any guarantees about what will happen here, or in another company you might move to."

"I understand there are no guarantees, but this is the first big economic downturn I've faced in my career. I know you've gone through a few ups and downs during your career. How did you decide when it was time to stay or go?"

"We've heard a lot that this crisis is unprecedented, like nothing that has happened in most of our lifetimes," he said. "And the current crisis is unique in many ways, but we've gone through tough times and challenging situations in the past."

"I would be interested to know how you made those decisions in the past, recognizing that each situation is unique and ultimately I have to make my own choices," Sam said.

"Well, then, with your permission, I'll share a couple of examples from my experience that illustrate some principles that might be useful to you. At the foundation," Lou began, "it comes back to a question we often ask in coaching, and that is What do you want? or What are your goals in the current situation? I've been in tough situations in the past where I decided to stay and fight for survival and situations where I decided to move to something else that had risks of its own.

"In one case I joined a consulting firm shortly before an economic downturn. Several consultants were laid off among a couple dozen of us in our local office. Two had less time in the company than I had, and one who had been there longer but worked in an area that had declining revenue even before the downturn. In my mind, I thought that I could easily be the next one to go if the tough times continued," Lou said.

"My assessment," Lou explained, "was that the company was sound although we needed to trim costs and make other adjustments. In that case, I decided to stay and redouble my efforts. I started volunteering for more projects, traveling more to support work in other offices, and learning other parts of the business. I was able to ride out the tough times and actually progress to more responsible roles. I ended up having a long and fulfilling tenure in that firm!"

"I love to hear that," Sam said.

"In another case, though," Lou began, "the crisis came unexpectedly and again I had fairly short tenure in my position. In that case I felt I was in a vulnerable spot. I didn't believe the company was on a solid footing, and I didn't have a high confidence level in the boss I was working for. So I decided to look for new opportunities, even though changing jobs brought risks of its own."

"What did you do?" Sam asked.

"I found an organization that needed the skills and experience I had, although I'd never held exactly that job title. It involved doing work in an internal training and development position. I had a wonderful experience in the organization I went to and actually continued on the same path with several companies over the next ten years.

"And there you have it!" Lou concluded. "Two situations with similar challenges, but my assessment of the risks and rewards took me in two very different directions. And I don't know to this day if either decision was right or wrong. I just know that I was able to move forward successfully with the path I chose in each case."

"That doesn't surprise me about you, Lou," Sam responded. "I appreciate the two examples, and your experience gives me confidence that I can choose my own path, which may or may not be right for someone else in the same circumstances."

"It's an individual decision in each situation, that's for sure," Lou agreed. "And I'd like to believe that if the path I chose hadn't worked out, I would have been flexible enough to try something else that would have worked. For me there's also an element of faith, or trust in a Higher Power—God who directs my steps on the path I choose (from Proverbs 16:9)."

"I appreciate that, and I know that reliance on the spiritual dimension is a perspective we share," Sam said gratefully. "It will be interesting to see where the current situation takes us in the months to come."

Reflection:
Find the Takeaway

There are cycles up and down in business and in life. After a time of strengthening her skills and growing as a leader through the program in her company and her MBA, Sam and the rest of her organization have gone through a trying time triggered by larger economic changes. Even now there is a lot of uncertainty about how this might work out and how long the current challenges last.

Yet Sam appears to be centered in her strengths and engaged in community with her team, her organization, and others in her life who support and encourage her.

While it doesn't alter the reality of the challenges she is experiencing, these elements contribute to her resilience and enable her to persist through the hard times.

What will you remember from all of this that will help you not only meet the challenges you will face as a leader but also grow from them?

Questions for Personal Reflection and Group Discussion

1. What are some difficult or unexpected situations you've gone through previously in your life and career? How did you get through them? What was the result? Consider how you used your strengths, EI, and resilience.

2. What's going on today that is presenting you with unforeseen challenges or affecting the plans you had for your life and career in some way? How are you addressing these current circumstances? What more could you do?

3. Who do you know who is a leadership coach, colleague, or business leader who could support you through a process of considering how to deal with current and impending challenges? Continue the process of building on your strengths, expanding emotional intelligence, and enhancing your resilience—it's a lifetime journey!

14

Three Years in the Future

"I'm now starting my tenth year of working with leadership development at ATA, and I'm grateful for the long-standing relationship we've had with your senior leaders here, and their input to keep the program fresh and relevant," Lou said to a new group of participants in the Next Gen program.

"And sometimes I have the very rewarding experience of having a past program participant come to do the kickoff for a new group. And that's the case today. Please welcome Samantha Denton, Director of Customer Service."

Most of the participants clapped courteously, with a few enthusiastic call-outs from those who had worked with or for Sam.

"Sam, you came through the program about four years ago, when you were a manager in customer service. And you've been the director now, how long?" Lou asked.

"About two years now," Sam said, adding, "I not only participated in an earlier version of this program, but also had Lou as a coach, which was one of the most helpful components." She looked directly at Lou for a moment. "And I remember something you told us is that our development as a leader is never done."

Turning back to the group, Sam continued, "Since the Next Gen program, I've completed my MBA, and I actually considered leaving ATA when we went through so many challenges with the economic downturn a few years ago. I talked to a lot of people to learn from the wisdom of their experience."

With a quick glance in Lou's direction, she continued, "Of course no one could tell me what I needed to do. But I saw our leaders working hard to secure the company's future, and I believed I had skills and experience to contribute and help the organization through a tough time. Since then we've grown, organically and by acquiring some competitors before they went out of business. Some of you here today may have come from one of those companies that were acquired, and collectively you've added value to the culture and performance of our company." She smiled at a few faces in the group.

"One of the lessons I've learned through this time is how much I still have to learn as a leader," Sam affirmed. "Every job change, leading at a higher level, or even having new job responsibilities can all bring new challenges and opportunities." Sam paused.

"Opportunity," she said slowly and deliberately. "That was the term my director used when he told me I'd be attending this program four years ago. I wasn't so sure. In fact, I almost tried to talk him out of putting me in the program at that time. But he believed that I was ready and seemed confident that I could balance being in the program with my job responsibilities as well as family and outside interests. His support helped me to take the next step and join the program.

"Some of you may be having some of the same thoughts. I can assure you, there's no time like the present when it comes to your professional development as a leader. I'm glad I got into this program when I did and had the opportunity to complete it. That timing opened up another job opportunity when the company reorganized, and then ultimately brought me back to take my director's role in customer service when he was promoted. And his path was similar to mine, which shows that there is plenty of opportunity within our company to grow and advance if you're prepared."

Lou chimed in, "That word, *opportunity*, is somewhat of a dual-edged sword. You felt the challenge of taking on one more thing when you started the program four years ago. But I hope everyone noticed how many times you used the word *opportunity* in a very positive way as you described the advancements that have happened in your career since you came through this program, completed your MBA, and put your knowledge and skills to work in new ways when the company went through challenging times."

With modesty, Sam said, "I would have never dreamed this is where I would be today when I started the Next Gen program, but everything fell in place because people saw potential and willingness in me to take on more, and I've had strong teams working with me in every role I've had in our company.

"That can be the case for you, too, if you'll apply yourself fully to the opportunity that is in front of you now," Sam concluded. "Stay focused, apply yourself, and you're going to achieve greatness."

This time the applause for Sam was louder and more sustained, and Lou knew this new group was off to a strong start, thanks to Sam.

Closing Reflection:
Your Best Self at Work

Sam has the opportunity to recall the people, programs, and processes that contributed to her development as a leader and to pay it forward to a new group of aspiring managers in the same program. Her ability to remember how she felt at the beginning and how her perspective changed as a result of her experiences and interactions set the stage for others to make the choice to invest their own time and effort in a process that is just starting for them. And Sam shows that she is continuing to grow in her perspective and leadership potential.

Can you project yourself out? Imagine yourself three years into the future. Maybe even ten years. Visualize, sense, and feel what you will be like. Bring together the best of your strengths, emotional intelligence, and resilience. Imagine facing challenges. Imagine how the current problems and difficulties you are facing can be the seed or fertilizer for your future growth in leadership and character. What do you notice? What is it about your current personality, talents, and skills that hold the potential for you to create your best self at work?

Summary of
Key Terms and Concepts

Here's a quick review of major concepts discussed in the book relating to professional development of your strengths, emotional intelligence, and resilience to support being your best self at work. These descriptions appeared as sidebars in the chapters where each term was first discussed.

Competencies and Skills (Chapter 3)

Competencies (or Leadership Competencies). A competency is often defined as the quality or state of having sufficient knowledge, judgment, skill, or strength; and competency enables one to then perform and carry out a task with some effectiveness. In *Your Best Self at Work*, we focus on four broad competencies labeled as Head, Heart, Hands, and Feet. These refer, respectively, to skill sets of making decisions, connecting with people, getting things done, and driving change. Many professions and training programs use competency-based models or frameworks to define the core qualities needed in a job or profession. Leadership competencies include many diverse qualities described in this book, including personal and social competence, emotional intelligence, and resilience.

Skills. A skill is a proficiency or ability to act, think, or communicate with a defined level of success or expertise and is acquired or developed through training or experience. Individuals may have strong potentials (strengths) that inform and shape their skills. Also, the more we use skills over time, the more they become strengths. In *Your Best Self at Work*, we discuss skills as components of the four broad competencies of Head, Heart, Hands, and Feet. In addition, skills can be either *intra*personal, within oneself (for example, self-knowledge), or *inter*personal, involving interaction with others (such as communication).

Self-Leadership and Growth Mindset (Chapter 3)

Self-Leadership. The concept of self-leadership was developed by management scientist Charles Manz who defined it as a self-influence process through which people achieve the self-direction and self-motivation necessary to perform. Research identifies three types of self-leadership strategies: (1) behavior-focused attempts to be more self-aware and regulate ourselves in situations, especially challenging ones; (2) natural reward behaviors where we try to create situations that are motivating, enjoyable, and especially intrinsically rewarding; and (3) developing constructive thought patterns or ways of thinking and attitudes that can positively impact our performance. Being your best self at work requires self-leadership.

Growth Mindset. The idea of growth mindset comes from the work of Carol Dweck at Stanford University and her colleagues. In its most basic essence, a growth mindset refers to the idea that we view our talents and abilities not as fixed entities but as expandable commodities that can always grow. This is in contrast to a fixed mindset where we believe that we are relatively set and unchangeable to any extent. This rich, multifaceted research has demonstrated, for example, that having a growth mindset actually makes it more likely that people will be prepared to change and will show a significant increase in their abilities over time.

Talents & Strengths (Chapter 5)

Talents. Talents and strengths are often used interchangeably, but there's an important difference. Talents refer to "raw capabilities" or a person's tendency to think, feel, or act in a particular way, based on personality traits or other characteristics. Thus, most "strength assessments" might be better titled as "talent identifiers." Talents become strengths when a person gains knowledge, skills, and experience (practice) to help refine and develop their talents.

Strengths. Strengths refer to talents which have been developed into a set of skills and behaviors that improve a person's performance and results. Leadership strengths are personal qualities and characteristics within individuals that allow them to become better leaders over time. Strengths represent the positive potential everyone has to use, develop, and leverage their own specific talents with and for other people (including groups, teams, and organizations) in order to help others to get in touch with their own strengths, for the purpose of fulfilling some mutual goal or objective.

Strength Themes and Realms (Chapter 5)

Strength Themes. Themes reflect a pattern of behaviors that tends to recur as a person makes their way in the world, with others, and in our jobs. Most strength assessments include two to three dozen themes (typically grouped into a handful of realms, as described below). A theme may look and sound different from one person to another as that theme interacts with other themes and personal characteristics of each individual. Within the history, story, or narrative of an individual life and career, there is a tendency for strengths, talents, and skills to repeat over and over across different situations. The ability to discern strength themes often comes with experience and age and can also be facilitated through coaching and assessments.

Strength Realms. A realm refers to a particular grouping of different strength themes. Specifically, a realm is a set of strength themes that share certain characteristics and tendencies in common. Realms are often used to help members of a team identify and understand similar themes in others. For example, one person might have a theme of personal goal accomplishment while another might have a strength in organizing others to perform a task or project together. Both themes could be part of a realm that describes getting things done. One popular strength assessment uses four realms (or domains) that were derived statistically—strategic thinking, executing, relationship building, and influencing. Other assessments use a more conceptual or logical grouping of themes, such as the VIA Inventory of Strengths with twenty-four themes grouped into six "virtues."

Thus there is a hierarchy of strengths: (1) Realm is the broadest category of similar strength themes; (2) Themes refers to a pattern of specific strengths that might look similar from one person to another; and (3) Individual strengths are the most specific set of skills and behaviors that constitute a person's unique approach to work and leadership.

Personality (Chapter 5)

Personality is typically defined as the complex of characteristics that distinguishes an individual from others; it is the total set of tendencies and predispositions that make someone distinctive or unique. The total personality of an individual includes many of the qualities discussed in this book: strengths, talents, values, and emotions. Personality provides the foundation for our behaviors, skills, and competencies as observed by others. However, personality is a broader concept and is defined in different ways through diverse theories and models. Research on personality traits suggests that these traits can be categorized into five different factors (called the Big Five): openness, conscientiousness, extraversion, agreeableness, and emotional stability.

Emotional Intelligence or EI (Chapter 6)

EI refers to a set of skills and behaviors that can be developed and improved in the areas of understanding and navigating the emotional experiences in oneself and others. EI is the capacity to be aware of, control, and express one's emotions, and to handle interpersonal relationships judiciously and empathetically. EI has four components: self-awareness, self-management, social awareness, and relationship management. Emotional intelligence supports us in being our best self at work, and, as emotionally intelligent leaders, we can support and even help bring out the best self of others at work.

Resilience (Chapter 10)

Resilience is the ability to not only bounce back from stress and adversity but also the ability to transform the stress experience into a learning experience and, hence, provides a basis for thriving in the future. For many, resilience entails significant adversity and even trauma. Resilient leaders are those who have faced and overcome failures and, through that experience, are better able to serve and bring out the strengths of their teams. Following the writings of coauthor Joel Bennett (author of *Raw Coping Power*), resilience contains five qualities that reside within individuals and teams, the Five Cs: centering, confidence, commitment, compassion, and community. These qualities may also be strengths.

Character and Values (Chapter 10)

Character (as in "a person of character"). Character "applies to the aggregate of moral qualities by which a person is judged apart from intelligence, competence, or special talents," if you examine a dictionary definition. In other words, a person can have qualities of virtue, goodness, moral soundness, integrity, and authenticity as aspects that are independent of talent or the ability to perform. We use character in *Your Best Self at Work* because, for some individuals, their best self may be due more to their overall moral character than to strengths, skills, or talents.

Values. Put simply, a value is a standard or principle that one considers worthwhile or worth pursuing or upholding in word, behavior, and lifestyle. Very often, our best self at work emerges when we decide what is most important and meaningful and then behave in ways that align with those values.

Unifying Concepts: Alignment and Best Self (Chapter 12)

Alignment. Alignment has a particular meaning in *Your Best Self at Work* and refers first to the coordination or finding connections between our strengths and emotional intelligence (EI). While certain strength realms link to specific EI skills, we can use *any* strength to develop any area of EI, and we can use our EI to assess whether we should express ("dial up") or downplay ("dial down") a strength within a particular situation or interaction. We learn to adjust, arrange, and calibrate how we express our strengths and EI in order to bring our best self to work. Alignment also includes integrating strengths, EI, and resilience together. For example, through adversity we become stronger and can also better lead others as we use EI to discern which of our strengths helps us overcome particular challenges.

Best Self. The idea of best self comes from the notion that effective leaders know how to bring out the best in others. This means helping people to be true to their values and facilitating conditions that bring their full set of strengths and express their full talents, skills, and competencies. One's best self may also be expressed through resilience, following adversity. The overall purpose of this book is to help you bring your best self to work.

Bonus Feature:
50 Tips for Uncertain Times

Application Points for Job Seekers, Career Changers, and Unemployed and Underemployed Workers

Our story takes place in the context of an organization and the career of a young manager, highlighting what we consider to be best-practice, evidence-based development programs. But we realize the world of work is experienced by many people in ways that are much different than this.

You may be struggling just to survive in the current challenging economic conditions driven by the global pandemic of 2020–2021, as well as the political turmoil and continued racial injustice in our nation and around the world. You may be seeking a job because you lost one or your current position is no longer providing a livable wage. You may feel forced to find another career path, or you may have used the experiences of the past year to reassess where you are and where you want to be, resulting in a change of direction.

We believe the underlying principles of growth and development in this book can be applied by anyone in any phase of their life and career. Whether you're just starting out or starting over, aiming for the next step in your career or changing to an entirely different path, these principles will serve you well.

These tips also serve as a supportive review of key points from the book to apply regardless of your current circumstances. We believe that you will find at least one from the 50 tips we offer here that can help you with these uncertain times.

Tips for Ongoing Growth, Learning, and Positive Development on Your Best Self Journey

1. **Foster a growth mindset**. Many people operate from a fixed mindset where they feel that they have only a limited set of resources, talents, and capabilities. They view failure as final and limiting. People with a growth mindset know they can build new skills and knowledge to become more effective, and failure is just an opportunity to learn how to do something better next time.

2. **Keep learning**. Seek opportunities to gain new skills and knowledge for personal and professional growth. These learning opportunities—training classes, job aids, resources—often happen within companies but can also be accessed at little or no cost through your local community college, workforce development agencies, and online resources.

3. **Seek feedback**. Ask others you trust for feedback to get better. A simple format that makes it easy to give and receive constructive feedback is to ask people to complete two sentences for you with regard to your skills and behavior: (a) "You are effective because—," and (b) "You would be even more effective if—." Ask several people and listen for common themes and ideas you can put into action.

4. **Lead yourself first**. Self-awareness and self-leadership are major themes in our book. Remember that you need to first apply the lessons you're learning to yourself before you'll be ready to go and help support others.

5. **Acknowledge your own best practices**. Write down several examples of past success when you did something you enjoyed doing, did it well, and had a feeling of satisfaction and fulfillment from doing it. Look for the common themes of skills, behaviors, and motivations that describe you at your best. Be prepared to share those examples in job applications and interviews so others can truly see you at your best.

6. **Implement the HHHF framework**. Consider the framework of head (thinking), heart (feeling), hands (doing), and feet (changing). While each of us can do all of those things, we tend to be naturally drawn to one (or maybe two) of those over the others in our baseline orientation to work and life. Which one do you lead with? How could you put that to use and do it even more in your present circumstances?

7. **Pinpoint behaviors from the HHHF framework**. This book describes the four broad realms of strengths as thinking, relating, doing, and persuading (similar to the four categories of skills listed above: head, heart,

hands, and feet, respectively). Which of the four realms tends to be your focus most of the time? What are examples of the specific talents or strengths you employ within this realm?

8. **State your aspiration**. Write a statement that summarizes "the kind of leader I want to be." (You can substitute "professional" or "worker" if you're not aiming to be in a leadership or management job right now, although we believe all of us have opportunities every day to be leaders and influencers.) This is a statement of aspiration, a profile of you at your best— your best self at work! Keep your statement in a place where you will see it regularly and be reminded about the person you are becoming.

Tips for Finding Support and Camaraderie on Your Best Self Journey

9. **Cultivate friendship**. Find someone to talk with about the challenges you're experiencing. A true friend is always willing to listen and be with you through the difficulties you're facing. Listen back.

10. **Find allies**. Who's on your team? Even if you're unemployed or underemployed, chances are there are current or previous bosses, peers, and coworkers, as well as friends and family members, who know you and want the best for you. Actively recruit them; ask them to be a part of your team to support you in your goals for a new job, a better job, greater use of your skills, or your specific goal.

11. **Hang with a mentor**. Who do you know who could be a mentor or coach for you today? What opportunities

do you have to learn from them? Consider a phone call, sharing a meal, taking a walk, or just sitting down for a conversation together. Don't look for just one perfect mentor; realize that you can learn different skills from many people. Make it a regular practice to spend time with others you can learn from.

12. **Meet up**. Ask others to join you in reading a book (like this one!), taking a class, or finding videos and other resources online that provide new lessons and examples for a challenge you share in common. Share the resources with each other and meet regularly to discuss how to put the ideas into practice.

13. **Emulate the best in strengths**. Who is the best leader you have personally known or worked for? What strengths made them a great leader? What did they do or say that had a positive influence on you? In what ways do you want to be like them? What will you do today to think, speak, and act more like this person? What strengths are being expressed?

Tips for Assessment and the Inward Part of Your Best Self Journey

14. **Assess for growth**. What are some of the assessments and surveys you've completed in the past that helped you understand yourself better? What areas would you like to understand about yourself better? Chances are good that you can find free assessments online, in addition to those provided in this book, to help you gain new insights about yourself and begin to grow in new ways.

15. **Take a strengths assessment**. Complete an assessment of your strengths such as the free Values in Action

Inventory of Strengths (VIA-IS) at https://www.viacharacter.org/.

16. **Study your results**. Study the results of your strength assessment(s); read more about the themes that emerge; talk to others about your results. These steps will help you to be more purposeful and intentional about using and building on your strengths.

17. **Highlight the positive self**. Describe your personality. While that may sound like a difficult task, people talk about personality characteristics all the time. Think of three or four *positive* words or phrases people have used when describing you (for example, organized, passionate, steady, creative). Write these down.

18. **Highlight what needs changing**. If there was one thing you could change about your personality or behavior, what would it be? Each of our personal characteristics gives us positive aspects to utilize and negative tendencies to avoid or overcome. You don't necessarily change your personality, but you can change your behavior to be more effective. And yes, write this one down too.

19. **Bring strengths into job application**. Your strengths should be clearly expressed and highlighted in every job application you submit, in your resume (if required in your field), and in responding to questions in job interviews. Practice with a friend or coworker to ensure you can share clear and concise examples of your strengths in action.

Tips for Emotional Intelligence (EI): General

20. **Remember emotional intelligence.** Assess your ability to understand emotions in yourself and others, and to manage your own emotions as well as managing interactions with others in the context of emotions. These four aspects are the essence of emotional intelligence. Everyone has it to some degree, and most of us need to use it more.

21. **Identify EI areas needing growth.** Emotional intelligence is a skill set we all can continually improve on. After assessing where you're starting from, consider where you most need to improve. This is often easiest to determine in the context of a specific situation or challenge you're dealing with. Identify specific behaviors you want to change and skills you want to gain.

22. **Get to know the best in EI.** Consider others who do well with different aspects of emotional intelligence (self-awareness, self-management, social awareness, and relationship management) and learn from them. Observe their behavior and, if you have the opportunity, ask them to describe how they deal with different situations.

Tips for EI Self-Awareness

If you're working to improve or enhance your self-awareness of emotions and how they affect you, consider these suggestions:

23. **Learn to name the emotions you're feeling in order to deal better with them.** If you're struggling to put your emotions into words, think about how emotions are expressed in music, movies, and books. These

examples can help you understand and be able to better express how you feel.

24. **Identify the things that trigger the emotions you feel.** Know your early warning signs, especially for negative emotions. Identify people and situations that "push your hot buttons" and get you into a bad state of mind.

25. **Examine your values.** What are the beliefs you live by (such as responsibility and equity) and the end-states you work to achieve (wisdom, love, happiness)? Write down your top five to seven values. Assess how well you're living those values in how you spend your time and your money.

26. **Know your strengths and limitations**, especially as it pertains to interactions with others and dealing with challenging situations.

Tips for EI Self-Management

If your focus is on improving self-management in an emotional context, apply these ideas:

27. **Count to ten silently** when you feel the rush of adrenaline in an emotional or difficult situation (the fight, flight, or freeze response). This gives your rational brain time to catch up with the emotional reaction you're feeling and helps ensure you don't say or do something that you'll be sorry for later.

28. **Practice self-control in your self-talk** and how you express emotions to others in words and actions. Talk about what you're feeling rather than taking direct action.

29. **Make sure you're getting enough sleep, good nutrition, and other factors** that keep your mind and body healthy and able to deal with the challenges you face.

30. **Use your planning and organizing skills** to make a plan and follow through in addressing troubling emotions or past difficulties, whether these emotional circumstances are immediate or long-standing.

Tips for EI Social Awareness

If you want to get better at awareness of emotions in others, consider these ideas:

31. **Work on reading facial expressions and body language** for greater awareness of when others are experiencing negative emotions.

32. **Practice active listening.** Be attentive, block out distractions, lean into conversations, maintain good eye contact, and give good verbal feedback (like "mm's" and "ah's") to let others know you are tracking with what they're saying.

33. **Ask people you trust to tell you when they become aware of difficult emotions** in others around you so you can learn to be more aware and empathetic.

34. **Learn to ask questions** about what emotions other people are feeling and how they're coping with difficult situations. Your efforts to better understand others and their emotions, if done sincerely, will help them see you as empathetic.

Tips for EI Relationship Management

If you want to get better at managing relationships in emotional circumstances and difficult situations, try these steps:

35. **Take time to analyze a past situation or interaction** with others that didn't go well and learn from it. Reconstruct what happened, what you were thinking, what was said, and the impact it had. Determine where things went wrong and decide what you will do differently in similar situations in the future.

36. **Look for opportunities to be part of a team** in order to enhance your communication and influence skills. Even if you work mostly alone, recognize that we are social beings and can benefit from talking with others and learning from them.

37. **Use a range of approaches** in dealing with conflicts and negotiations, working to strike a balance between understanding where others are coming from and asserting your own point of view. Most people will appreciate your perspective more if they know you're also hearing their concerns and issues. Seek first to understand, then to be understood.

38. **Aim to be a positive influence with others** in your words and behavior, especially when others are struggling with emotional circumstances. When you make a decision, tell others the "why" behind your decision or action so they can better understand your values and motives.

Tips for Aligning EI and Strengths

39. **Use your strengths to help you develop and refine your EI** for greater effectiveness in your work. Each of the four strength realms can give you a firm cornerstone in EI. Specifically, strengths in the thinking realm support the skills of self-awareness and personal insight. Strengths in the doing realm align with and support self-management. Relating strengths provide a foundation in social awareness and empathy, and influencing strengths give a head start on the skills of relationship management, including influence, negotiation, and conflict management.

40. **While understanding the alignment above is important, you can use any (and all) of your strengths to develop skills in any of the four areas of emotional intelligence,** as well as other skills you may want to develop or improve. Use the strengths you have to accomplish the things you want to do.

41. **Also, use your EI to regulate the best application of your strengths.** Learn when to dial up or dial down a strength based on the situation and the people with whom you're interacting. This will help ensure your strengths don't become weaknesses through overuse or misapplication.

Tips for Cultivating Resilience and the Five Cs of Resilience

42. **Let stress teach you.** Hardship is, well, hard, but still can be an excellent teacher. Many people look back and express that their times of greatest growth came through the most difficult times of their lives. What

kinds of trials and difficulties have you been through, and what have you learned? Keep good notes (literally, write things down) to remind yourself in the future of what you've learned and how far you've come. Consider purchasing Dr. Bennett's book *Raw Coping Power: From Stress to Thriving*, which includes over thirty exercises for cultivating resilience.

43. **Use daily reminders, affirmations, and songs that inspire**. There are dozens of aphorisms or positive sayings that help us when we get bogged down by stress and adversity. For example, "When life hands you lemons, set them on fire," or "When the going gets tough, the tough get going." Find your favorite and keep it posted near you or on your phone as a reminder. Similarly, find songs or other inspiring affirmations and use them when you need to.

44. **Play up your Five C strength**. From your review and assessment of each of the Five Cs, determine which one is your strongest and ask others what they would say about you. Do the same for them. Whether it is centering, confidence, commitment, compassion, or community, we each can identify with at least one and help others do the same.

45. **Spend time with other Five C people**. At the same time, identify which of the Five Cs needs development in you. Seek out others whom you feel are good in that area and just spend time talking to them about how they have developed that in themselves. Really listen. For example, "How did you get so good at staying calm in crisis?" (centering) or "What makes you keep focused and persevering even when there are

so many obstacles?" (commitment). Very often, these conversations can be powerful for both you and them.

46. **Cultivate team resilience in your family**. During difficult times (like with the pandemic or political strife), it can help to sit down with members of your family and have them each take the Five C assessment in this book. Have each person go around and give examples of when they saw how a behavior in a family member demonstrated one of the Five Cs. Share positive appreciation and think about family activities that will help grow those qualities even further. Give everyone a chance to talk.

47. **Be mindful of mental health**. While all the tools, assessments, and tips in this book are geared to bringing out your best self, it is important to also remember your limits when it comes to potential problems with mental health. Depression, anxiety, substance abuse, personality problems, suicidal thinking, serious relationship conflict—these may require the help of a mental health professional. Make sure you reach out for help as there is a lot available. Most communities, churches, schools, and workplaces offer help. The US Department of Health & Human Services has a 24/7 mental health helpline: 1-800-662-HELP (4357).

Tips for Alignment of Strengths, Emotional Intelligence, and Resilience

48. **Be creative about "The Best of the Best."** The great thing about the many resources and strengths described in this book is that you have many to choose from. Specifically, as you read and reflect on all the

topics covered, ask yourself, "Which particular story, tool, or topic most resonated with me?" and "Which strength, EI area, or Five C was THE ONE that I can definitely say is a core strength?" Treat that area as a totem or anthem in your life. You can imagine it as a coat of arms or a code of excellence or credo that you draw from, write about, or make a poem about.

49. **Contemplate the give-and-take.** We believe that strengths, EI, and resilience constantly work together. When one area lacks, another one comes in for support. When life gets particularly difficult, all three areas sort of team up to help. Reflect on a time in your life (perhaps now) where you can see how these all work together to make you strong.

50. **Write to us.** We would love to hear from you about which of these tips you found particularly helpful. When you take a moment to share your story with us, the authors, it has a certain solidifying or crystallizing effect on your strength. Also, other areas start to come into focus. We bet that when you take that step to share your story, you will also notice how complementary resources come into play. For example, if you write about one of the Five Cs of Resilience, you might notice how the HHHF framework, and EI area, or a particular strength is also part of the story. You can contact us at www.YourBestSelfAtWork.org.

End Notes

Chapter 1

Readiness for Growth. There are many career paths of leaders as well as many factors that motivate leaders to grow, develop, and become their best self. A significant body of research describes these paths and motivations. Just using Sam as an example, we see her desire to stay positive despite challenges, the need for support and mentoring, the motivation to make the right decision, and also the desire to be true to herself or authenticity.

This book makes the central assumption that all leaders have a central organizing motivation: the desire to develop the best in themselves and to express this central self in the service of a higher principle, typically serving the greater good. Each of Sam's desires relates to or is served by this "best self" aspiration.

To learn more about leadership motivation and how it may shape one's career, please consider these articles and books. Of particular interest for "best self" motivation, readers might consider the book by Neck and Manz (2010), the dissertation by Yan (2011), and the special issue of *The Leadership Quarterly* (Avolio & Gardner, 2005).

Avolio, B. J., & Gardner, W. L. (2005). Authentic leadership development: Getting to the root of positive forms of leadership. *The Leadership Quarterly, 16*(3), 315–338.

Higgins, M. C., & Kram, K. E. (2001). Reconceptualizing mentoring at work: A developmental network perspective. *Academy of Management Review, 26*(2), 264–288.

Komives, S. R., & Wagner, W. (Eds.) (2016). *Leadership for a Better World: Understanding the Social Change Model of Leadership Development.* John Wiley & Sons.

London, M. (2001). *Leadership Development: Paths to Self-Insight and Professional Growth.* Psychology Press.

Neck, C. P., & Manz, C. C. (2010). *Mastering Self-Leadership: Empowering Yourself for Personal Excellence.* Pearson.

Yan, W. (2011). *Eudaimonic orientation: The pursuit of the best self* (Doctoral dissertation, University of Missouri–Columbia).

Chapter 2

The Next Gen Leadership Program. The Next Gen program, while fictitious, represents a synthesis of business school and corporate leadership programs. Many students ask whether these programs are effective. Research from dozens of studies suggests that while programs can be highly effective, they may not always be so, and effectiveness often depends on the right combination of factors and the right fit between the student or manager and the program (e.g., Collins & Holton, 2004; Lacarenza, et al., 2017; Reyes, et al., 2019).

The current story attempts to bring in some factors that research suggests contributes to effective leadership development. Speaking generally, this includes making the program voluntary to reinforce intrinsic motivation, identifying student needs beforehand, providing feedback, using multiple delivery methods (especially giving students a chance to practice), conducting spaced training sessions and face-to-face delivery, and making the effort to match training examples to actual job situations. It also involves providing coaching (MacKie, 2016).

More specifically, in regard to bringing out one's best self, we focus on training and coaching that could bring out one's strengths, talents, or authentic self. Also, studies on authentic leadership show that it is an important predictor of positive outcomes at work. While the study of actual authentic leadership training is new (e.g., Nübold et al., 2020; van Droffelaar & Jacobs, 2018), a wealth of studies on positive leadership, ethical leadership, and servant leadership shows these to be very promising (Cunha et al., 2020).

Collins, D. B., & Holton III, E. F. (2004). The effectiveness of managerial leadership development programs: A meta-analysis of studies from 1982 to 2001. *Human Resource Development Quarterly, 15*(2), 217–248.

Cunha, M. P. E., Rego, A., Simpson, A., & Clegg, S. (2020). *Positive Organizational Behaviour: A Reflective Approach*. Routledge.

Lacarenza, C. N., Reyes, D. L., Marlow, S. L., Joseph, D. L., & Salas, E. (2017). Leadership training design, delivery, and implementation: A meta-analysis. *Journal of Applied Psychology, 102*(12), 1686-1718.

Nübold, A., Van Quaquebeke, N., & Hülsheger, U. R. (2020). Be(com)ing real: A multi-source and an intervention study on mindfulness and authentic leadership. *Journal of Business and Psychology, 35*(4), 469–488.

Reyes, D. L., Dinh, J., Lacarenza, C. N., Marlow, S. L., Joseph, D. L., & Salas, E. (2019). The state of higher education leadership development program evaluation: A meta-analysis, critical review, and recommendations. *The Leadership Quarterly, 30*(5), 1–15.

van Dam, K., van der Locht, M., & Chiaburu, D. (2013). Getting the most of management training: the role of identical elements for training transfer. *Personnel Review, 42*(4).

van Droffelaar, B., & Jacobs, M. (2018). Nature-based training program fosters authentic leadership. *Journal of Leadership Studies, 12*(3), 7–18.

Chapter 3

Head, Heart, Hands, and Feet. The idea that good leaders utilize multiple aspects of their self or personality—and as a whole person—is not new. In the late seventeenth century, the Swiss educational reformer, Johann Heinrich Pestalozzi, used the "head, hands, and heart" model as a central approach to developing the child as a whole person (cf. Brühlmeier, 2010).

The idea was later extended to leadership development by Nicholls (1994) and has been used as a general guide for managerial practice, including at Google (see Shah, 2015). Although the concept is discussed here as four separate skills, it is important to keep in mind that, as the person matures into a whole "best" self, all four are integrated and work together to bring out a higher state of wholeness and well-being (Dunn, 1961).

Brühlmeier, A. (2010). *Head, heart and hand: Education in the spirit of Pestalozzi*. Open Book Publishers.

Chua, R. Y. J., Ingram, P., & Morris, M. W. (2008). From the head and the heart: Locating cognition- and affect-based trust in managers' professional networks. *Academy of Management Journal, 51*(3), 436–452.

Culp III, K., & Cox, K. J. (1997). Leadership styles for the new millennium: Creating new paradigms. *Journal of Leadership Studies, 4*(1), 3–17.

Dunn, H. (1961). *High-Level Wellness: A Collection of Twenty-Nine Short Talks on Different Aspects of the Theme "High-Level Wellness for Man and Society"*. Arlington, VA: Beatty.

Nicholls, J. (1994). The "heart, head and hands" of transforming leadership. *Leadership & Organization Development Journal*, 15(6), 8-15.

Shah, R. (2015). Engaging employees in their feet, heart and head. (November 27, 2015). *Forbes* online.

Self-leadership. The concept of self-leadership, as discussed here, is based on the original work of Charles Manz (1986), which has resulted in a significant body of research. A simple definition of self-leadership is the process by which a person influences themselves to achieve their aims in life. The book by Christopher Neck and colleagues (2019) is an ideal place to start for a practical understanding with case studies. The self-leadership questionnaire (Houghton & Neck, 2002) and a brief version (Houghton et al., 2012) can also be found through Google Scholar. Examples (and dimensions) from these items include the following:

- I establish specific goals for my own performance (self-goal setting).

- I picture in my mind a successful performance before I actually do a task (visualizing performance).

- I talk to myself (out loud or in my head) to work through difficult situations (evaluating beliefs and assumptions).

Houghton, J. D., & Neck, C. (2002). The revised self-leadership questionnaire: Testing a hierarchical factor structure for self-leadership. *Journal of Managerial Psychology*, 17(8), 672–691.

Houghton, J. D., Dawley, D., & DiLiello, T. C. (2012). The abbreviated self-leadership questionnaire (ASLQ): A more concise measure of self-leadership. *International Journal of Leadership Studies*, 7(2), 216–232.

Manz, C. C. (1986). Self-leadership: Toward an expanded theory of self-influence processes in organizations. *Academy of Management Review, 11*(3), 585–600.

Neck, C. P., & Houghton, J. D. (2006). Two decades of self-leadership theory and research: Past developments, present trends, and future possibilities. *Journal of Managerial Psychology,* 21(4), 270–295.

Neck, C. P., Manz, C. C., & Houghton, J. D. (2019). *Self-Leadership: The Definitive Guide to Personal Excellence.* Sage Publications.

Stewart, G. L., Courtright, S. H., & Manz, C. C. (2011). Self-leadership: A multilevel review. *Journal of Management, 37*(1), 185–222.

Growth Mindset. Carol Dweck's work on growth mindset has been discussed broadly in the business literature. Employees who have a growth mindset or strong learning orientation are more likely to be engaged at work, find greater meaning in their jobs, have competence in their knowledge and skills, and show self-determination in making a strong impact on their work unit and organization (see Baek-Kyoo et al., 2019). It is not only possible to encourage a growth mindset in students (Yeager et al., 2019), doing so may be the foundation for bringing out one's best self.

Baek-Kyoo, J. B., Bozer, G., & Ready, K. J. (2019). A dimensional analysis of psychological empowerment on engagement. *Journal of Organizational Effectiveness: People and Performance,* 6(3), 186–203.

Dweck, C. (2012). *Mindset: Changing the Way You Think to Fulfill Your Potential.* Hachette UK.

Dweck, C. (2016). What having a "growth mindset" actually means. *Harvard Business Review, 13,* 213–226.

Yeager, D. S., Hanselman, P., Walton, G. M., Murray, J. S., Crosnoe, R., Muller, C., ... & Dweck, C.S. (2019). A national experiment reveals where a growth mindset improves achievement. *Nature, 573,* 364–369 (2019).

Chapter 4

Leadership Coaching. The field of leadership and executive coaching has grown exponentially in recent years. Coaching differs from broader leadership development programs (like the fictional Next Gen program in this book), which uses more "baked in" curriculum and exercise. Leadership coaching is a one-to-one or individualized and customized process that attends to the specific career and work context of the individual and has been shown to improve self-reported leadership skills.

We recommend the book by MacKie (2016) on strengths-based leadership coaching. MacKie provides guidance on several factors associated with effective coaching that also help to bring out one's best self. This includes ensuring the coach is adequately trained and prepared, using self-assessments, obtaining assessments from multiple raters (360-degree feedback), assessing readiness, using tailored goal setting, and providing feedback, accountability, and challenges.

Bozer, G., & Jones, R. J. (2018). Understanding the factors that determine workplace coaching effectiveness: A systematic literature review. *European Journal of Work and Organizational Psychology, 27*(3), 342–361.

Ely, K., Boyce, L. A., Nelson, J. K., Zaccaro, S. J., Hernez-Broome, G., & Whyman, W. (2010). Evaluating leadership coaching: A review and integrated framework. *The Leadership Quarterly, 21*(4), 585–599.

MacKie, D. (2014). The effectiveness of strength-based executive coaching in enhancing full range leadership development: A controlled study. *Consulting Psychology Journal: Practice and Research, 66*(2), 118-137.

MacKie, D. (2016). *Strength-Based Leadership Coaching in Organizations: An Evidence-Based Guide to Positive Leadership Development.* Kogan Page Publishers.

Rekalde, I., Landeta, J., Albizu, E., & Fernandez-Ferrin, P. (2017). Is executive coaching more effective than other management training and development methods? *Management Decision, 55*(10), 2149–2162.

Chapter 5

Strength Assessments. As the chapter explains, there are different approaches to assessing strengths in personality and in leadership and through the lens of positive psychology. Here are a few of the most popular ones:

a. Gallup's CliftonStrengths® assessment (previously StrengthsFinder®): This is a personality-based instrument that measures talent in four domains of strategic thinking, executing, relationship building, and influencing. The standard assessment gives a person their Top 5 Themes (from thirty-four possibilities) and costs $20 on Gallup's website; there is also an All 34 Themes report available for a cost of $50. Someone who has a Top 5 Report can upgrade to the All 34 report for $40. Gallup Certified Strengths Coaches receive a discount of $10 on each of these assessments. Contact author Ben Dilla (who is Gallup certified) through our website, YourBestSelfAtWork. org, if you would like to take this assessment, upgrade a previous report, or discuss your results.

b. The VIA Inventory of Strengths (VIA-IS), formerly known as the Values in Action Inventory, is a 240-item measure of twenty-four character strengths grouped into six factors or virtues (wisdom/knowledge, courage, justice, humanity, temperance, and transcendence). While there are some parallels to the four domains of CliftonStrengths®, the VIA framework is more conceptual and not based on statistics. The online assessment with basic report (rank ordering of the twenty-four themes) is free. The Top 5 Report with in-depth analysis of your signature strengths is $19, and

Total 24 report, including analysis by virtue categories is $49. There is also an option for a Team Report with Top 5 Strengths of three to fifteen individuals on a team for $15 per person. https://www.viacharacter.org/

c.   Strengths Profile (previously known as the Realise2 Inventory) is an online self-assessment that provides feedback on sixty possible strengths, dividing them into your realized strengths, unrealized strengths, learned behaviors, and weaknesses. The sixty strengths are also grouped into five strengths families, which include being, communicating, motivating, relating, and thinking. The Introductory Profile costs $14, the Expert Profile is $40, and a Team Profile is $110. https://strengthsprofile.com

d.   StandOut 2.0 (and the original StandOut) was developed by Marcus Buckingham, who was also instrumental in developing Gallup's CliftonStrengths® assessment. This assessment uses thirty-four situational judgment questions to assess eighteen talents which are paired together into nine strength roles. The report provides your rank order of all nine with a focus on your top two roles (primary and secondary) and how they work together. You can purchase the assessment online for $15 or buy the book for about the same cost, including a key code for the assessment. https://standout.tmbc.com/purchaseassessment

e.   Strengthscope® was developed in Europe and is used globally. The model has twenty-four strengths divided into four groups (relational, execution, thinking, and emotional) similar to the four CliftonStrengths® domains. The standard self-assessment report provides results on all twenty-four strengths (graphed in a circle with your strengths as spokes, shown in comparison to their normative group) and a focus on your Significant 7 top strengths. Strengthscope offers multiple options besides the standard individual report, including a 360-degree feedback profile, a leadership profile, and a team report. You must purchase

Strengthscope from a certified practitioner; see website for costs, which are comparable to other strength assessments: https://www.strengthscope.com/

f. Qualitative 360/Reflected Best Self Exercise™: For a completely different approach, you could do a Qualitative 360 by asking colleagues, friends, and others who know you well to identify your main talents and strengths and analyzing their feedback for common themes that define "your best self." There is a proprietary tool, the Reflected Best Self Exercise™, developed by scholars at the Center for Positive Organizations at the University of Michigan, which requires permission to use or payment of $75 to use their platform, https://reflectedbestselfexercise.com/. No permission is needed to use a Qualitative 360 process as described here; the process has been published in *Harvard Business Review* and *Academy of Management Journal* and is in the public domain. Please contact Ben Dilla if you want more details or would like him to facilitate the process of gathering your feedback.

The references that follow provide a sample of some key source texts for the interested reader. The chapter by Rashid (2015) provides a thorough introduction on assessments and the book by Simmons and Lehmann (2012) is a compendium of dozens of strengths-based assessment tools. The four-factor model and corresponding assessment used in this chapter represents an elementary attempt to synthesize these models for the purpose of providing a basic orientation and introduction to readers. More rigorous studies may be found by following up on the references provided here.

Donaldson, S. I., Lee, J. Y., & Donaldson, S. I. (2019). Evaluating positive psychology interventions at work: A systematic review and meta-analysis. *International Journal of Applied Positive Psychology*, 4, 113–134.

Fredrickson, B. L. (2001). The role of positive emotions in positive psychology: The broaden-and-build theory of positive emotions. *American Psychologist, 56*(3), 218-226.

Hodges, T. D., & Clifton, D. O. (2004). Strengths-based development in practice. *Positive Psychology in Practice, 1,* 256–268.

Peterson, C., & Seligman, M. E. (2004). *Character Strengths and Virtues: A Handbook and Classification* (Vol. 1). Oxford University Press.

Rashid, T. (2015). Strength-based assessment. In *Positive Psychology in Practice: Promoting Human Flourishing in Work, Health, Education, and Everyday Life, Second Edition,* 519–542.

Simmons, C., & Lehmann, P. (2012). *Tools for Strengths-Based Assessment and Evaluation.* Springer Publishing Company.

Youssef, C. M., & Luthans, F. (2007). Positive organizational behavior in the workplace: The impact of hope, optimism, and resilience. *Journal of Management, 33*(5), 774–800.

The Big Five Model of Personality Traits. Otherwise known as the Five-Factor Model, this well-studied and popular approach to understanding personality first examines those attributes, traits, or adjectives that people use to describe themselves and others and then derives the most basic categories to cluster those traits. The model was originally credited to Tupes and Christal (1961) and then more fully developed by McCrae and Costa (1987).

Regarding leadership, the Big Five is understood as a dispositional approach—that is, the claim is sometimes made that we can fully understand and explain leadership behavior by reference to the internal disposition or character of an individual. A key question in this research is "What type of leadership relates to the Big Five?" For example, one meta-analysis suggests that the Big Five may not be sufficient for understanding transformational leadership (Bono & Judge, 2004). Importantly, this study consistently found that transformational leadership measures correlated negatively with neuroticism and positively with extraversion. This analysis contrasts with studies of ethical leadership, which found that conscientiousness plays the most important role (Kalshoven et al., 2011).

Further, studies have shown that openness to experience may be the best predictor of success or greatness among US presidents (Rubenzer et al., 2000; Simonton, 2006). These disparate findings point to two ideas. First, one's best self as a leader may be expressed through different traits and in different contexts. Second, neuroticism either does not relate to effectiveness or can be a detriment.

Bono, J. E., & Judge, T. A. (2004). Personality and transformational and transactional leadership: A meta-analysis. *Journal of Applied Psychology, 89*(5), 901-910.

Judge, T. A., & Bono, J. E. (2000). Five-factor model of personality and transformational leadership. *Journal of Applied Psychology, 85*(5), 751-765.

Kalshoven, K., Den Hartog, D. N., & De Hoogh, A. H. B. (2011). Ethical leader behavior and big five factors of personality. *Journal of Business Ethics, 100,* 349–366.

McCrae, R. R., & Costa, P. T. (1987). Validation of the five-factor model of personality across instruments and observers. *Journal of Personality and Social Psychology, 52(1),* 81–90.

Rubenzer, S. J., Faschingbauer, T. R., & Ones, D. S. (2000). Assessing the US presidents using the revised NEO Personality Inventory. *Assessment, 7*(4), 403–420.

Simonton, D. K. (2006). Presidential IQ, openness, intellectual brilliance, and leadership: Estimates and correlations for 42 US chief executives. *Political Psychology, 27*(4), 511–526.

Tupes, E. C., & Christal, R. E. (1961). Recurrent personality factors based on trait ratings (USAF ASD Tech. Rep. No. 61-97). Lackland Air Force Base, TX: US Air Force.

Chapter 6

Emotional Intelligence. Early psychologists such as E. J. Thorndike in the 1920s had theories about social intelligence, and Gardner's (1983) concept of multiple intelligences included both intrapersonal intelligence (knowing oneself) and interpersonal intelligence (understanding feelings and emotions in others).

Contemporary interest in the topic traces back to Daniel Goleman's (1995) book, *Emotional Intelligence*, as well as Goleman's (1998a) article in *Harvard Business Review*, "What makes a leader?" which tied the concept directly to leadership effectiveness. We recommend Goleman's (1998b) book *Working with Emotional Intelligence* for a thorough discussion of workplace applications. Also, *Emotional Intelligence 2.0* by Bradberry and Greaves (2009) provides a very accessible discussion of the four facets of EI discussed here and includes an online assessment with strong face validity and practical suggestions for improvement of each facet of EI.

A key distinction in the research literature is between trait EI and ability-based EI, although measurement of the latter has proven to be problematic (Petrides, 2011). We use EI here in both senses—first, as a trait-like construct that people possess in varying degrees and also as a set of skills and behaviors that can be developed and improved, based on research evidence (Mattingly & Kraiger, 2019).

Bradberry, T., & Greaves, J. (2009). *Emotional Intelligence 2.0*. TalentSmart.

Gardner, H. (1983). *Frames of Mind: The Theory of Multiple Intelligences*. Basic Books.

Goleman, D. (1995). *Emotional Intelligence*. Bantam Books.

Goleman, D. (1998a). What makes a leader? *Harvard Business Review, 76*, 93–102.

Goleman, D. (1998b). *Working with Emotional Intelligence*. Bantam Books.

Mattingly, V., & Kraiger, K. (2019). Can emotional intelligence be trained? A meta-analytical investigation. *Human Resource Management Review, 29*(2), 140–155.

Petrides, K. V. (2011). Ability and trait emotional intelligence. In T. Chamorro-Premuzic, S. von Stumm, & A. Furnham (Eds.), *The Wiley-Blackwell Handbook of Individual Differences* (p. 656–678). Wiley-Blackwell.

Chapter 7

Strength-based Leadership. The book *Strengths Based Leadership* by Rath and Conchie (2008) has stimulated both applied and basic research into strengths for leadership, including case studies (Welch et al, 2014) and quantitative studies (e.g., Kong & Ho, 2016). The edited volume by Oades et al. (2017) and textbook by Cunha et al. (2020) provide extensive references for a broader analysis of strength-based approaches at work.

Cunha, M. P., Rego, A., Simpson, A., & Clegg, S. (2020). *Positive Organizational Behaviour: A Reflective Approach*. Routledge.

Ho, Violet T., and Dejun Tony Kong (2016). A self-determination perspective of strengths use at work: Examining its determinant and performance implications. *The Journal of Positive Psychology, 11*(1), 15–25.

Oades, L. G., Steger, M., Delle Fave, A., & Passmore, J. (Eds.). (2017). *The Wiley-Blackwell Handbook of the Psychology of Positivity and Strengths-based Approaches at Work*. John Wiley & Sons.

Rath, T., & Conchie, B. (2008). *Strengths based leadership: Great leaders, teams, and why people follow*. Gallup Press.

Welch, D., Grossaint, K., Reid, K., & Walker, C. (2014). Strengths-based leadership development: Insights from expert coaches. *Consulting Psychology Journal: Practice and Research, 66*(1), 20-37.

Chapter 8

The Five Cs of Resilience. The Five Cs were originally developed by Bennett and Aden (2011) following a synthesis of the literature on personal resilience and then applying those concepts to a formulation of team resilience (Bennett et al., 2010; 2018). In a meta-analysis of resilience interventions, Leppin et al. (2014) stated that the Five Cs framework is supported theoretically. A more comprehensive model of resilience, consistent with the Five Cs, is described in Bennett (2018; 2020) and Hartmann et al. (2020).

Bennett, J. B. (2018). Integral Organizational Wellness™: An evidence-based model of socially inspired well-being. *Journal of Applied Biobehavioral Research, 23*(4), e12136.

Bennett, J. B. (2020). Resilience 3.0: Multi-level approaches are essential. *Worksite Health International. 11*(3), 8–13.

Bennett, J. B., & Aden, C. (2011). Team resilience: Health promotion for young restaurant workers. In Bray, J.W., Galvin, D.M., & Cluff, L.A., Eds. *Young Adults in the Workplace: A Multisite Initiative of Substance Use Prevention Programs.* RTI Press Publication No. BK-0005-1103. RTI Press.

Bennett, J.B., Aden, C. A., Broome, K., Mitchell, K., & Rigdon, D. (2010). Team resilience for young restaurant workers: Research-to-practice adaptation and assessment. *Journal of Occupational Health Psychology, 15*(3), 223–236.

Bennett, J. B., Neeper, M., Linde, B. D., Lucas, G. M., & Simone, L. (2018). Team resilience training in the workplace: E-learning adaptation, measurement model, and two pilot studies. *JMIR Mental Health, 5*(2), e35.

Hartmann, S., Weiss, M., Newman, A., & Hoegl, M. (2020). Resilience in the workplace: A multilevel review and synthesis. *Journal of Applied Psychology, 69*(3), 913–959.

Leppin A. L., Bora P. R., Tilburt, J. C., Gionfriddo, M. R., Zeballos-Palacios, C., Dulohery, M. M., et al. (2014). The efficacy of resiliency training programs: A systematic review and meta-analysis of randomized trials. *PLoS ONE 9*(10), e111420.

Acknowledgments

Ben: I would like to thank all of the people who helped shape me into the person I am today, although there are too many to name. They would include teachers who inspired and challenged me; leaders in the US Air Force who influenced me as a young officer and helped me to grow as a man of faith; business executives who were my leaders, colleagues, and clients; academic colleagues who set a high standard in teaching, research, and service; and friends and family members who have supported me and my family over the years.

I'm especially appreciative of the love and support from my wife, Sharon, and our three adult children and their spouses/partners: Steven and Emily, Nathan and Amanda, and Kristen and Drew.

Specifically with regard to the ideas contained in this book, I thank my colleagues at Personnel Decisions International (now Korn Ferry), both in the Dallas operating office and at our headquarters in Minneapolis, who contributed to my growth as a consultant, training facilitator, and coach and who influenced the approaches I utilize today in professional development.

I'm grateful to those who have helped train and mentor me as a leadership coach, including David B. Peterson, Blanca Estela Garcia, Casandra Fritzsche, Mina Brown, Peggy Dean, Meg Rentschler, Brent O'Bannon, Julia Stewart, and Donna Zajonc.

I'm thankful for the opportunity to teach in the Gupta College of Business at The University of Dallas and the wonderful example of all of my faculty colleagues, especially those who teach in the leadership and management curriculum: Rosemary Maellaro, Jude Olson, Julia Fulmore, Cara Jacocks, J. Lee Whittington, Dale Fodness, and Greg Bell.

My colleagues and friends in the Dallas–Fort Worth Organizational Development Network (DFW ODN) and the North Texas chapter of the International Coaching Federation (ICF-NT) were instrumental in the refinement of many of the ideas expressed here through their feedback on formal presentations as well as informal dialogue about these ideas. In particular, I appreciate the input and encouragement of Jim Jameson, Pete Sorenson, Michele Studer, Beth Guyton, Terri Adkisson, Pallavi Ridout, Christina Bell, Ed Savage, and Nila Sinha.

For over a dozen years now, I've been blessed by the fellowship and encouragement of a group of like-minded men in monthly meetings, book discussions, social activities, and individual friendships. What started out as "five guys sitting around talking" became what we now know as a mastermind group, and I consider all of the current members to be my personal board of directors. Their interest, encouragement, and accountability were instrumental to me in finishing the book, and their comments on earlier versions of the manuscript were very important in shaping what you're now reading. My sincere thanks go to Daryl Thomas (our organizer and leader from the start), Dan Mohr, Craig Holloway, Luis Escalante, Preston Dunn, Tom Riney, Kiran Hosahalli, and Jim Davis.

Having Joel Bennett join me as a coauthor was an even greater help than I imagined in the refinement and expansion of these ideas and their presentation in a way that invites personal reflection and application by readers. Thank you for being a mentor, role model, and friend.

Our editor, Sandra Wendel, helped transform our manuscript to a more polished and readable form. Also, her advice and recommendations for the many tasks of publication were invaluable.

Finally, I appreciate the graduate students and workshop participants who served as beta readers and provided essential feedback to improve the storyline and presentation of ideas. (At the same time, Joel and I take full responsibility for the expression of those ideas in this book.) Special thanks go to Joan Bradee, Esmeralda Axler, Andy Farley, Mallori DeSalle, and Zach Eckert for their helpful comments.

I am a better person because of the influence and support of these people and many more. Thank you!

Joel: My intellective contributions to this book would not have been possible without the original (and early) education and collegial discussions I have had with key people in two areas: leadership and resilience.

Regarding leadership, I have to first thank those individuals who were on my dissertation committee from the University of Texas at Austin (1985), starting with my dissertation chair, Dr. Janet Spence, and others on the committee, Drs. Don Baumann, Joseph Horn, Robert Helmreich, and Larry Browning. By the recollection of that time of seminal support, I also thank Dr. Cristina Banks and Dr. June Gallesich for teaching me about organizational processes that set the stage for further learning about real power and influence in leadership.

Regarding resilience, I have to acknowledge all those involved in our original Team Resilience research that was funded by the Substance Abuse & Mental Health Services Administration through the leadership of Dr. Deborah Galvin and the partnership with Carlson Restaurants Worldwide/TGI Fridays® (KC Cunningham, Katherine Taylor-Gadsby, Mike Archer). Charles ("Chuck") Aden was the central person on our team who helped me formulate the Five Cs of Resilience model featured in this book.

I am ever grateful for my wife, Jan, who supports me in the more important emotional and spiritual resources that allow me to contribute to such wonderful creative endeavors as this. Finally, here is to the honor of knowing and working with my coauthor, Ben.

About the Authors

Benjamin L. Dilla, PhD

Ben is an executive coach, trainer, and consultant through Bold Leader Development (BLD LLC) and a business professor in the Satish & Yasmin Gupta College of Business at The University of Dallas.

He served as an aircraft maintenance officer, behavioral scientist, and personnel officer in the US Air Force, as a senior leadership development consultant for Personnel Decisions International (now Korn Ferry), and in organizational development and training leadership roles for several organizations based in the Dallas–Fort Worth area, including Fannie Mae, American Airlines, UT Southwestern Medical Center, and Parkland Health & Hospital System.

As a coach, Ben often works with accomplished professionals to develop and improve their leadership and influence skills, which led him to promote a strengths-based approach to the skills of emotional intelligence and resilience.

Ben is an Associate Certified Coach (ACC) through the International Coaching Federation (ICF), Board Certified Coach (BCC) through the Center for Credentialing and Education (CCE), and Gallup Certified Strengths Coach, and he has been certified in Marshall Goldsmith's Stakeholder Centered Coaching (SCC) process.

Ben earned a bachelor of science degree in behavioral sciences and leadership from the US Air Force Academy and his MS and PhD in industrial and organizational psychology from Purdue University. He has written or coauthored over twenty peer-reviewed research articles and professional conference presentations. Ben is an active member of the Dallas–Fort Worth Organizational Development (OD) Network and the North Texas chapter of the International Coaching Federation.

Joel B. Bennett, PhD

Joel is president of Organizational Wellness & Learning Systems (OWLS), a consulting firm in North Texas that specializes in evidence-based wellness, resilience, mental well-being, and catalyzing healthy work cultures from the inside out.

Joel trains people, facilitators, coaches, and consultants in areas related to resilience, workplace well-being, a soulful orientation toward time, and interpersonal mindfulness.

He first delivered stress-management programming in 1985, and OWLS programs have since reached close to 250,000 workers across the United States and abroad. OWLS clients include corporate, private, nonprofit, local, and federal agencies. OWLS has received close to $5 million in federal research grants to assess, design, and deliver workplace wellness programs.

In 2008, Joel's work was recognized with the Service Leadership Award from the National Wellness Institute. He earned his bachelor's degree in psychology and philosophy from State University of New York (Purchase) and his MA and PhD in psychology from the University of Texas at Austin.

He is the author of over thirty peer-reviewed research articles, and he has written or coauthored five books including *Raw Coping Power*.

Made in the USA
Las Vegas, NV
15 October 2021